James Patience is a barrister at Hundred Court chambers. He specialises in clinical negligence, personal injury, and inquest work. He acts for both Claimants and Defendants and has considerable experience of claims arising out of fatal accidents both in the context of being led and as sole junior. He provides lectures and training to solicitors, barristers and health professionals on many aspects of the law relating to damages arising from torts.

A Practical Guide to Claims Arising from Fatal Accidents

Third Edition

A Practical Guide to Claims Arising from Fatal Accidents

Third Edition

James Patience
Barrister-at-Law
Hundred Court Chambers

Law Brief Publishing

Published 2026 by Law Brief Publishing, an imprint of Law Brief Publishing Ltd
30 The Parks
Minehead
Somerset
TA24 8BT

www.lawbriefpublishing.com

Paperback: 978-1-918241-26-6

To Esther Patience

PREFACE

Claims for damages following a fatal accident are almost always upsetting for the client and can be complex and difficult for the lawyer. They must be dealt with by the practitioner with empathy, accuracy and an eye for detail.

The law in its current state is a combination, at times uneasy, of statutory law and common law legal principles. The statutory framework has its origin in "jury award" cases of the 19th century. Various aspects of the statutory framework have been updated sporadically over the years, but many learned commentators consider that there remain aspects of the legal framework which still merit revision to bring the law in line with modern values. The combination of statutory and common law principles, the large number of factual variables and the fluid nature of calculating losses means that awards in this area can often seem unusual to even the most experienced practitioner.

This book aims to provide an easily accessible resource for both the practitioner new to the area and for the experienced personal injury lawyer. It aims to be a clear guide to all the legal principles necessary for running a claim for damages following a fatal accident, from examining the cause of action to apportioning an award of damages.

Thank you to Bryn Auger (Hundred Court Chamber's civil pupil) for assisting with the research.

The law in this book is described as believed to be correct at 1st January 2026.

James Patience
Hundred Court Chambers
January 2026

CONTENTS

CHAPTER ONE

THE HISTORICAL BACKGROUND TO THE PRESENT LEGISLATION

1.1 INTRODUCTION

In this chapter the development of the current statutory framework for damages for wrongful death is examined. The current statutory framework is summarised.

1.2 THE HISTORIC COMMON LAW POSITION

In the past there was no right of action in tort in English law which enabled a claimant to recover damages for the wrongful death of another[1].

The origin of this position at common law can be traced to the case of *Baker v Bolton*[2] which was determined in 1808. This case concerned the death of the plaintiff's wife in a coach accident. The portion of the claim that was concerned with damages flowing from the death of the plaintiff's wife, failed. Lord Ellenborough summarised the position at common law as it was at the time:

1 At Scottish law the Court could grant a solatium to the bereaved family for grief.

2 (1808) 1 Camp 493

> *In a civil Court, the death of a human being could not be complained of as an injury; and in this case the damages, as to the plaintiff's wife, must stop with the period of her existence.*

Before the decision in *Baker,* it is difficult to identify a clear authority for this proposition. The principle enunciated by Lord Ellenborough was subsequently confirmed by the Court of Appeal in *Admiralty Commissioners v SS Amerika*[3].

Subsequent decisions demonstrate that this rule was absolute. It was not possible in the case of *Baker* for a husband to recover damages for the death of his wife; neither was it possible for a parent to recover damages for the death of their child,[4] nor an employer for the death of his employee[5].

In addition to the "rule from *Baker v Bolton*", with a very few exceptions[6], the maxim of *actio personalis moritur cum persona* (a personal action dies with the person) also operated.

1.3 LORD CAMPBELL'S ACT

The combination of the rule from *Baker v Bolton* and the maxim of *actio personalis moritur cum persona* created a position which was unsatisfactory. The situation was such that if a person were injured through a tort, the wrongdoer would be liable for causing the injury but if that person were killed through the same tort there was no liability. There was a very limited exception to this position whereby the

---

3 [1917] A.C. 38

4 Clark v London General Omnibus Co [1906] 2 K.B. 648

5 Osborn v Gillett (1873) L.R. 8 Ex 88

6 Exceptions to this rule arose where the deceased had appropriated property. In these circumstances the rightful owner of the property could maintain an action against the deceased's estate.

deceased's estate had available to it an action in contract[7] but this was of limited use.

As a result of the increase in fatal accidents on England's developing rail network parliament acted to correct this position by enacting a statute[8]. The Fatal Accidents Act 1846, popularly known as "Lord Campbell's Act" (which was enacted in the face of some opposition from the railway industry) gave the right to personal representatives of the deceased to bring a legal claim for damages on behalf of the husband, parent, or child of the deceased.

1.4 CONSOLIDATION AND REFORM TO THE PRESENT DAY

The Law Reform (Miscellaneous Provisions) Act 1934 amended the law further so that if the injured person survived for any period of time and had a right to sue for injury, this right was preserved on death and could be pursued by the estate of the deceased.

Over the years the Fatal Accidents Act 1846 was amended and eventually consolidated in the Fatal Accidents Act 1976[9]. The Fatal Accidents Act 1976 itself was amended by the operation of the Administration of Justice Act 1982 which expanded the categories of individuals entitled to claim for damages.

The Fatal Accidents Act 1976 and the Law Reform (Miscellaneous Provisions) Act 1934 constitute the framework of statutory law that gives

7 See Jackson v Watson & Sons [1909] 2 K.B. 193 where a wife died from food poisoning from food purchased by her husband. The husband successfully recovered, in a claim for breach of contract, for the loss of her services.

8 Hansard 21 August 1846, Vol 88, col 926

9 There were further Fatal Accidents Acts in 1846, 1908 and 1959.

rise to awards of damages in relation to fatal accidents today. Each act gives rise to different considerations which are considered in detail below.

Recently, the Damages for Bereavement (Variation of Sum) (England and Wales) Order 2020 came into force on the 1st May 2020. This increases the sum awarded for bereavement damages. This is discussed in chapter 14.

The Fatal Accidents Act 1976 (Remedial) Order 2020 was (finally) enacted on 6 October 2020 and applies to all causes of action after that date. This order addressed the incompatibility of the Fatal Accidents Act with the European Convention of Human Rights by amending the Fatal Accidents Act to allow bereavement damages to be recovered by the cohabiting partner of the deceased. This is discussed in chapter 14.

1.5 SUMMARY

In summary:

a) Historically, at common law, there was no right of action which enabled a claimant to claim damages for the wrongful death of another;

b) Because of an increase in deaths on England's developing rail network this position was altered by the 1846 Fatal Accidents Act – "Lord Campbell's Act";

c) The 1846 Act was followed by a number of consolidating acts culminating in the current statute – the Fatal Accidents Act 1976;

d) The Law Reform (Miscellaneous Provisions) Act 1934 amended the law so that if the injured person survived for any period of time and had a right to sue for injury, this right was preserved on death and could be pursued by the estate of the deceased.

CHAPTER TWO

CAUSES OF ACTION

2.1 INTRODUCTION

In this chapter the essential characteristics of the main causes of action under the Fatal Accidents Act 1976 and the Law Reform (Miscellaneous Provisions) Act 19434 are set out. Other potential causes of action under the European Convention of Human Rights and other, industry specific, statues are briefly identified.

2.2 THE MAIN CAUSES OF ACTION

There are now two main causes of action for claiming damages for wrongful death which are different and distinct from each other.

1. Under the Fatal Accidents Act 1976 a claim arises out of the death itself. Under the Fatal Accidents Act 1976:

    a) A claim may be made on behalf of any dependant of the deceased for financial loss caused by the death;

    b) A claim may be made by the dependants for funeral expenses[10];

10 Dependants must come within the class of dependants set out in S1(3) of the FAA '76. Claims for funeral benefits do not require dependants to show that they had a reasonable expectation of pecuniary benefit. See chapter fifteen below for a full discussion of funeral expenses.

c) A limited class of relatives may claim the statutory bereavement award.

2. Under the Law Reform (Miscellaneous Provisions) Act 1934 a claim arises out of the right of action that the deceased would have had if they had survived.

   a) A claim may be made by the estate of the deceased for injury, loss or damage which could have been claimed by the deceased had they survived;

   b) This will include damages for the deceased's past losses up to his death including their pain, suffering and loss of amenity;

   c) A claim can also be made for funeral expenses.

2.3 OTHER CAUSES OF ACTION

In addition to these two main causes of action there can be a cause of action under the European Convention on Human Rights (hereinafter ECHR) where death has been caused by a public authority. Since 2nd October 2000 the courts have had the power to make an award in damages for breaches of certain articles of the ECHR. Article 2 of the ECHR covers the right to life and so courts can award damages for the breach of this article. Claims under the ECHR are relatively unusual. Claims under the ECHR remain possible in the Brexit transition period. This cause of action is discussed further at chapter eighteen.

In addition to these causes of action, in particular and limited circumstances, a cause of action may also arise from a breach of the relevant sections of the Coal Mining (Subsidence) Act 1991; the Railways (Convention on International Carriage by Rail) Regulations 2005 and the Carriage by Air Act 1961. Claims made under these acts are increasingly rare and a detailed examination of these Acts is beyond the scope of this book. The main features of these statutes in relation to fatal accident claims are summarised in chapter nineteen.

2.4 SUMMARY

In summary:

a) The Fatal Accidents Act 1976 and;

b) The Law Reform (Miscellaneous Provisions) Act 1934 are the main causes of action in cases involving fatal accidents;

c) There may also be a potential cause of action under the European Convention on Human Rights where the death has been caused or contributed to by a public authority;

d) In particular and limited circumstances a cause of action may also arise from the Coal Mining (Subsidence) Act 1991; the Railways (Convention on International Carriage by Rail) Regulations 2005 and the Carriage by Air Act 1961.

CHAPTER THREE

THE FATAL ACCIDENTS ACT 1976

3.1 INTRODUCTION

This Act is one of the main considerations for the practitioner when considering a claim for damages for wrongful death. The Fatal Accidents Act 1976 repealed the relevant provisions of the previous Fatal Accident Acts[11] and applies to any death occurring after the 1st of September 1976.

This chapter considers:

a) The cause of action created by Section 1 of the Fatal Accidents Act 1976;

b) Who is entitled to bring an action under the Fatal Accidents Act 1976 and;

c) The fact that one action is brought for all dependants.

3.2 SECTION 1 OF THE FATAL ACCIDENTS ACT 1976

Section 1(1) of the Act states:

Right of action for wrongful act causing death.

(1) If death is caused by any wrongful act, neglect or default which is such as would (if death had not ensued) have entitled the person

11 Fatal Accidents Acts 1846, 1908, 1959

> *injured to maintain an action and recover damages in respect thereof, the person who would have been liable if death had not ensued shall be liable to an action for damages, notwithstanding the death of the person injured.*

In the case of *Gray v Barr*[12] Lord Denning MR provided a typically succinct summary of the effect of S1(1):

> *If [the deceased] had lived, i.e., only been injured and not died, and living would have been entitled to maintain an action and recover damages – then his widow and children can do so. They stand in his shoes in regard to <u>liability</u>, but not as to <u>damages</u>*[13]

3.3 SECTION 2 OF THE FATAL ACCIDENTS ACT 1976

3.3.1 PERSONS ENTITLED TO BRING THE ACTION

S2 of the Fatal Accidents Act 1976 sets out who is entitled to bring the action. At S2(1) and (2) it states:

> *Persons entitled to bring the action.*
>
> *(1) The action shall be brought by and in the name of the executor or administrator of the deceased.*
>
> *(2) If—*
>
> *(a) there is no executor or administrator of the deceased, or*
>
> *(b) no action is brought within six months after the death by and in the name of an executor or administrator of the deceased,*

12 [1971] 2QB 554 at 569D

13 Emphasis as per the original judgment.

> *the action may be brought by and in the name of all or any of the persons for whose benefit an executor or administrator could have brought it.*

Where there is no executor or administrator, or a delay in appointing one, any dependant may bring an action after six months have elapsed. The definition of a dependant is discussed in detail at chapter six.

If a claim is brought by an administrator care should be taken to ensure that the claim is not brought before letters of administration are granted. In the past this produced a situation whereby the proceedings were a nullity, and the courts had no power to correct the error. In the more forgiving modern era of the Civil Procedure Rules ("hereafter "CPR"), CPR 17.4(4) and 19.4 allow the court to alter the capacity in which a claimant brings an action, even after the expiry of the relevant limitation period. Of course, the cost and increased stress that such an application would cause should be avoided if possible.

The position when a claim is brought solely on behalf of the estate of the deceased under Law Reform (Miscellaneous Provisions) Act 1934 is different. An action brought on behalf of a deceased's estate by a person as administrator who at the date of commencing the claim does not have a grant is a nullity and the CPR does not operate to "save" the action[14]. Claims brought under the Law Reform (Miscellaneous Provisions) Act 1934 are discussed in detail in chapter 16.

Where the action is brought by the executor of the deceased the capacity to bring an action vests in the executor upon death. The grant of probate is merely proof of the executor's status[15].

3.3.2 ONE ACTION

14 Haastrup -v- Okorie [2016] EWHC 12

15 Ingall v Moran [1944] KB 160

Only one action may be brought in respect of wrongful death. Section 2(3) of the Fatal Accidents Act 1976 states:

> *Not more than one action shall lie for and in respect of the same subject matter of complaint.*

The CPR actively encourages using a single set of proceedings to dispose of all claims that can be "conveniently disposed of in one set of proceedings"[16]. One set of proceedings should be used where there is a claim under both the Fatal Accident Act 1976 and a claim under the Law Reform (Miscellaneous Provisions) Act 1934. Similarly, one set of proceedings should be used where the same accident has given a dependant a claim in a personal capacity for personal injuries and a claim under the Fatal Accidents Act 1976 as a dependant.

One set of proceedings is issued for all dependants. The damages (apart from the bereavement award) are then apportioned according to the degree of pecuniary loss. Section 3(1) of the Act states:

> *In the action such damages, other than damages for bereavement, may be awarded as are proportioned to the injury resulting from the death to the dependants respectively.*

Although it is clear that the broad case-management powers given to the court by the CPR[17] now permit a dependant to be added to an action after the matter has commenced, it is preferable to avoid the cost and stress of such an application and clearly ascertain who are the relevant dependants that must be included before the action is commenced.

Although alternative approaches are technically possible, by far the most usual approach is that the damages in a claim under the Fatal Accidents Act 1976 are assessed as a whole in the first instance and then apportioned

16 See CPR 7.3

17 See CPR 3 and 19

as appropriate in accordance with the loss suffered by each dependant[18]. Apportionment is discussed in more detail at chapter twelve.

3.4 INFORMING THE DEFENDANT

Whichever entitled party brings the action, S4 of the Fatal Accidents Act 1976 makes it clear that the defendant must be fully informed of the action and on whose behalf it has been commenced. S4 states:

> *The plaintiff in the action shall be required to deliver to the defendant or his solicitor full particulars of the persons for whom and on whose behalf the action is brought and of the nature of the claim in respect of which damages are sought to be recovered.*

3.5 SUMMARY

In summary:

a) Section 1(1) of the Fatal Accidents Act 1976 sets out the cause of action;

b) A claim may be brought by the executor or the administrator of the deceased's estate;

c) Where there is no executor or administrator, or a delay in appointing one, any dependant may bring an action after six months have elapsed;

---

18 See the dicta of Lord Guest in the case of Kassam v Kampala Aerated Water Co Ltd [1965] 1 W.L.R 668 at 672

d) If a claim is brought by an administrator care should be taken to ensure that the claim is not brought before letters of administration are granted;

e) Section 2(3) of the Fatal Accidents Act 1976 states that only one action may be brought in respect of wrongful death;

f) The defendant must be fully informed of the action and on whose behalf it has been commenced.

CHAPTER FOUR

THE NECESSARY ELEMENTS FOR A CLAIM UNDER THE FAA 1976

4.1 INTRODUCTION

To bring a claim under the Fatal Accidents Act 1976 the claimant must prove:

a) That the deceased person was injured by the wrongful act, neglect or default of the defendant;

b) That the deceased died as a consequence of that injury;

c) That at the time the deceased died he had a right to recover damages from the defendant;

d) That the dependants have suffered a loss as a result of the death.

It is clear that the claimant must prove every one of these elements otherwise the claim will fail[19]. The first three elements are discussed in detail below. The fourth essential element, and the issue of loss generally, is discussed in detail in chapter six.

19 As per Swift J in the case of Nunan v Southern Railway [1923] 2 KB 703 at 712

4.2 INJURED BY THE WRONGFUL ACT ETC.

This is rarely an area that causes great difficulty for the practitioner. For the sake of completeness, the following basic principles should be kept in mind:

a) The claimant must adduce evidence that establishes on the balance of probabilities that the deceased was injured by the wrongful act, neglect or default of the defendant;

b) If the deceased agreed to take on the risk of the accident himself in line with the legal maxim *volenti not fit injura* then the defendant will not have committed a wrongful act and there will be no cause of action[20];

c) The wording "wrongful act" covers a breach of statutory duty;

d) A breach of contract can amount to a "wrongful act, neglect or default"[21].

4.3. THAT THE DECEASED DIED AS A CONSEQUENCE OF THE INJURY

4.3.1 CAUSATION GENERALLY

The area of causation can prove more problematic. In particular this can be the case in instances of medical negligence where the death occurs against a background of other health problems. A full discussion of the concept of causation in tort law is beyond the scope of this book. What follows is a discussion of issues of causation that are particularly relevant to claims under the Fatal Accidents Act 1976.

20 Griffiths v Earl of Dudley (1882) 9 Q.B.D. 357

21 Grein v Imperial Airways Ltd [1937] 1K.B. 50

The usual rules of causation in tort apply in claims under the Fatal Accidents Act 1976. Accordingly, in a claim under the Act the claimant must prove that, on the balance of probabilities, the injury caused the deceased's death. The concept of material contribution operates in a claim under the Act just as it would in a claim for personal injury. In line with the normal principles of causation the injury need not be the only cause of death and damages can still be recovered where the deceased has contributed to their own death. The concept of contributory negligence is specifically provided for by S5 of the Fatal Accidents Act 1976.

Where the deceased has committed suicide as a result of a psychiatric condition caused by the defendant's breach then Damages may still be recovered under the Fatal Accidents Act 1976 Damages can still be recovered under the Fatal Accidents Act 1976 on behalf of dependants where one of the dependants has caused or contributed to the death of the deceased.

4.3.2 CONTRIBUTORY NEGLIGENCE

In the past contributory negligence was a complete defence to a claim for damages arising out of a fatal accident[22]. Now contributory negligence operates in the same fashion as in other tortious claims; the damages awarded are reduced according to the percentage that the party in question is held at fault.

Section five of the Fatal Accidents Act 1976 specifically deals with the concept of contributory negligence. It states:

> *Where any person dies as the result partly of his own fault and partly of the fault of any other person or persons, and accordingly if an action were brought for the benefit of the estate under the Law Reform (Miscellaneous Provisions) Act 1934 the damages recoverable would*

22 Senior v Ward (1859) 1 E. & E. 385; Nunan v Southern Railway [1924] 1 K.B. 223

be reduced under section 1(1) of the Law Reform (Contributory Negligence) Act 1945, any damages recoverable in an action under this Act shall be reduced to a proportionate extent.

4.3.3. SUICIDE

Wrongful acts, negligence and defaults that have caused or contributed to suicide are covered by the Fatal Accidents Act 1976. The House of Lords case of *Corr v IBC Vehicles*[23] clarified the law in this area and confirmed that damages can be recovered under the Act where the deceased had committed suicide as a result of suffering from depression because of the defendant's breach of duty.

In the case of *Corr* the deceased became acutely depressed because of an accident at the defendant's factory and committed suicide six years later. The House of Lords held that the deceased's suicide was a reasonably foreseeable consequence of the depression arising out of the accident for which the defendant was responsible. The deceased's act did not constitute a *novus actus interveniens*[24]. The case of *Pigney v Pointers Transport Ltd*[25] is another example of a case where the deceased committed suicide, but the court determined that his act did not break the chain of causation and found the defendant liable.

23 [2008] UKHL 13

24 A new intervening act that breaks the chain of causation.

25 [1957] 1 WLR 1121

4.3.4 SUICIDE AND CONTRIBUTORY NEGLIGENCE

In *Corr* there was no finding of contributory negligence. The House of Lords decided on the facts of the case in *Corr* that no blame could be attributed to the deceased. Lord Bingham stated:

> *For reasons already given, I do not think that any blame should be attributed to the deceased for the consequences of a situation which was of the employer's making, not his. Consistently with my rejection of arguments based on novus actus and unreasonable conduct, I would similarly absolve the deceased from any causal responsibility for his own tragic death. I would accordingly assess his contributory negligence at 0%. That, in my opinion, reflects the responsibility of the deceased for his own loss (see Reeves v Commissioner of Police of the Metropolis [1999] QB 169, 198).*[26]

The issue of contributory negligence was only addressed in the case of *Corr* with "*extreme brevity*"[27] and the finding is clearly one made on the (unusual and tragic) facts of that case.

In the case of *Reeves v Commissioner of Police of the Metropolis*[28] (referred to by Lord Bingham in his judgment above) the House of Lords took a different view. In that case a prisoner at risk of suicide had taken his own life. The House of Lords found that although the police had breached their duty of care in relation to the deceased, because the deceased had responsibility for his own life, he had also contributed towards his own death and a finding of contributory negligence could be made. Damages were reduced by 50%.

Perhaps it is needless to say that where there is no causal link between the defendant's wrongful act, neglect or default and the deceased's suicide no damages can be recovered. In the case of *Corr* Lord Bingham endorsed

---

26 *Corr* [2008] UKHL 13 at para 22

27 Ibid at para 19

28 [1999] 3 All ER 897

the logic that the British Columbia Court of Appeal applied in the case of *Wright v Davidson*[29] on this issue. He stated:

> *It is not fair to hold a tortfeasor liable, however gross his breach of duty may be, for damage caused to the claimant not by the tortfeasor's breach of duty but by some independent, supervening cause (which may or may not be tortious) for which the tortfeasor is not responsible. This is not the less so where the independent, supervening cause is a voluntary, informed decision taken by the victim as an adult of sound mind making and giving effect to a personal decision about his own future. Thus I respectfully think that the British Columbia Court of Appeal (McEachern CJBC, Legg and Hollinrake JJA) were right to hold that the suicide of a road accident victim was a novus actus in the light of its conclusion that when the victim took her life "she made a conscious decision, there being no evidence of disabling mental illness to lead to the conclusion that she had an incapacity in her faculty of volition: Wright v Davidson (1992) 88 DLR (4th) 698, 705.*

4.3.5 WHERE DEPENDANTS HAVE CONTRIBUTED TO DEATH

Where the negligence of a dependant has itself contributed to the death of the deceased then a similar concept to contributory negligence operates. That dependant's damages are reduced by the proportion which they are deemed to have been responsible for the deceased's death. The remaining dependants' damages are not reduced[30]. Where the negligence of one of the dependants has entirely caused the death of the deceased, that dependant cannot recover damages but the remaining dependants

29 (1992) 88 DLR (4th) 698, 705

30 Mullholland v McCrea [1961] N.I 135

are entitled to recover damages in their own right without any reduction[31].

4.4 SUMMARY

In summary:

a) To bring a claim under the Fatal Accidents Act 1976 the claimant must prove:

   i. That the deceased person was injured by the wrongful act, neglect or default of the defendant;

   ii. That the deceased died as a consequence of that injury;

   iii. That at the time the deceased died he had a right to recover damages from the defendant;

   iv. That the dependants have suffered a loss as a result of the death.

b) The claimant must prove every one of these elements otherwise the claim will fail;

c) Contributory negligence operates in the same fashion as in other tortious claims;

d) Damages can be recovered under the Fatal Accidents Act 1976 where the deceased had committed suicide subject to the normal concepts of reasonable foreseeability;

e) A reduction for contributory negligence is not inevitable where the deceased has committed suicide;

31 Dodds v Dodds [1978] Q.B. 543

f) Where the negligence of a dependant has itself contributed to the death of the deceased then that dependant's damages are reduced by the proportion which they are deemed to have been responsible for the deceased's death.

CHAPTER FIVE

RIGHT TO RECOVER

5.1 INTRODUCTION

In this chapter the legal basis of the cause of action under the Fatal Accidents Act 1976 is examined. Matters which exclude or limit a claim under the Act are discussed.

5.2 THE RIGHT OF ACTION AND PREVIOUS CLAIMS

The Fatal Accidents Act 1976 does not create a new right of action. This is apparent from the wording of the Act itself and is confirmed by the case law that followed the first Fatal Accident Act of 1846.

In the case of *Read v Great Eastern Railway Company*[32] the court emphasised that Lord Campbell's Act did not create a new cause of action. Referring to S2 of the Act on the assessment of damages Judge Blackburn states:

This section may provide a new principle as to the assessment of damages, but it does not give any new right of action.[33]

The principle set out in the case of *Read* was confirmed in the case of *Pickett v British Rail Engineering*[34].

---

32 (1868), L.R., 3 Q.B. 555

33 Ibid; See also Griffiths v. The Earl of Dudley (1882), L.R., 9 Q.B. 357, 363

34 [1980] A.C. 136

Because there is no new right of action conferred by the Act a claim will be barred if there has been a previous claim that has been brought and concluded by the deceased.

The case of *Pickett* has received (valid) criticism because of the relative chaos it created in the assessment of damages for "lost years" claims[35]. However, as things stand the cases of *Read* and *Pickett* remain good law in relation to previous proceedings being a bar to a further claim under the Fatal Accidents Act 1976.

In the case of *Thompson v Christine Arnold*[36] the claimant attempted to circumvent the decisions in *Read* and *Pickett* and persuade the court that the operation of Articles 6 and 8 of the ECHR meant that the law should be determined differently. However, the court confirmed that the case of *Read* remains good law and did not permit the claimant to bring an action for loss of dependency, an area of loss that had been deliberately (and negligently) omitted from the claim brought and settled in the deceased's lifetime.

Proceedings which are issued during the deceased's lifetime but then not served do not bar a claim under the Fatal Accidents Act 1976 from the dependants[37]. If the deceased has commenced proceedings which are then discontinued following death, it is not an abuse of process to start a further, new claim under the Fatal Accidents Act 1976[38]. Where a claimant dies before the conclusion of a claim, his or her dependants or personal representatives can be substituted as claimants in that action and continue the claim for their own losses[39]. Finally, it is clear from the

---

35 A situation that was eventually rectified by S4 of the Administration of Justice Act 1982 which amended S1 (2) of the Law Reform (Miscellaneous Provisions) Act 1934.

36 [2007] EWHC 1875 (QB)

37 Cachia v Faluyi [2001] WECA civ 998

38 Reader & ORS V Molesworths Bright Clegg [2007] EWCA Civ 169 2

39 Corr op cit.

wording of S3(2) of the Act that awards for provisional damages made in the lifetime of the deceased do not prevent a subsequent claim under the Fatal Accidents Act 1976[40].

5.3 AGREEMENTS TO LIMIT DAMAGES

If the deceased made an agreement to limit the amount of damages payable on their death this is not binding on the dependants for the purposes of a claim for dependency under the Fatal Accidents Act 1976. In the case of *Nunan v Southern Railway*[41] the deceased had made a contract which limited the amount of damages payable on his death to a certain sum. However, the court held that this agreement did not limit the amount of damages recoverable by his dependants under the Fatal Accidents Act.

5.4 ILLEGAL ACTS

The case of *Burns v Edman*[42] is an example of a case where the dependants' claim failed because the deceased had devoted his life to crime and was supporting his dependants with funds that had been derived from criminal offences. In that case it was determined that the action under the Fatal Accidents Act failed because of the operation of the principle of *ex turpi causa*. There is some criticism of the ratio of this decision as the dependants' cause of action for their loss of dependency did not itself arise from an illegal act. Nevertheless, claims where there is

40 In the case of Thompson op cit it was suggested to the claimant in the initial action that the matter would be better dealt with by a payment of provisional damages but this approach was not taken.

41 [1924] 1 K.B. 223 CA

42 [1970] 2 Q.B. 541

evidence that an element of the deceased's income came from illegal means should be treated with caution.

5.5 JURISDICTION

The Fatal Accidents Act 1976 creates a cause of action for the benefit of the dependants where the parties submit to the jurisdiction of the English courts, even if the death results from an incident outside English jurisdiction.

In the case of *The Esso Malaysia*[43] the dependants of a Russian seaman were permitted to bring a claim despite the collision in question concerning foreign ships which were outside English jurisdiction[44]. In the case of *Davidsson v Hill*[45], another case concerning a fatal accident at sea, the Court of Appeal confirmed that the dependants could pursue an action under Fatal Accidents Act despite the fact that the deceased was a foreign national.

More recently the case of *Brownlie v FS Cairo (Nile Plaza)*[46] the Supreme Court confirmed that the Claimants were permitted to issue their claim out of jurisdiction in England and Wales when the accident in question had occurred in Egypt. The case concerned the interpretation of the "gateway" test set out at CPR 6BPD.3 to serve proceedings out of jurisdiction and in particular the meaning of the wording "damage" found in sub paragraph 9 (a). The Court found there was no justification for restricting the meaning of "damage" to damage which was necessary to complete a cause of action in tort, or for according any special

43 [1975] QB 198, [1974] 2 All ER 705

44 Ibid

45 [1901] 2 K.B. 606

46 UKSC 45, [2022] A.C. 995

significance to a place simply because it was where the cause of action was completed.

5.6 LIMITATION

Limitation is an important consideration in fatal accident cases. A full discussion of the principles of limitation in this area along with extended extracts from the relevant statutes can be found at appendix B of this book. In summary:

In summary:

a) Where death is immediate the limitation period is usually 3 years;

b) Where the deceased was a minor the limitation period runs from their 18th birthday or from the date of death (whichever is sooner);

c) Where a dependant is a child their limitation period does not start to run until they are 18;

d) If the deceased was mentally incapable of bringing an action between the accident and the date of the death then the limitation period did not start to run in the deceased's lifetime;

e) Where the deceased has survived for a period of time after the accident and then died, a new three year limitation period commences on the day of death;

f) If the deceased survived for a period of longer than 3 years and no action was commenced then any action by his dependants after his death is time barred;

g) Particular care must be taken in regard to accidents at sea and accidents involving aircraft where, in certain circumstances, the limitation period is a strict 2 years;

h) Particular care must be taken if the accident has occurred abroad as the limitation period which prevails is the period of limitation in the jurisdiction where the accident occurs.

i) An application can be made under S33 of the Limitation Act 1980 to extend the limitation period. This application cannot be made in cases where the cause of action is under the Montreal Convention (Accidents involving aeroplanes) or the Athens Convention (accidents at Sea).

5.7 SUMMARY

In summary:

a) The Fatal Accidents Act 1976 does not create a new right of action;

b) A claim will be barred if there has been a previous claim that has been brought and concluded by the deceased;

c) If the deceased made an agreement to limit the amount of damages payable on their death this is not binding on the dependants for the purposes of a claim for dependency under the Fatal Accidents Act 1976;

d) Claims where there is evidence that an element of the deceased's income came from illegal means should be treated with caution;

e) The Fatal Accidents Act 1976 creates a cause of action for the benefit of the dependants where the parties submit to the jurisdiction of the English courts, even if the death results from an incident outside English jurisdiction;

f) Limitation is an important consideration (see Appendix B below for a full discussion).

CHAPTER SIX

THE DEPENDANTS' LOSS

6.1 INTRODUCTION

Usually the main focus of a claim under the Fatal Accidents Act 1976 is a claim for damages on behalf of the dependants of the deceased. The family members of the deceased seek to advance a claim to recover damages for the financial loss that they have suffered as a result of the death of their relative and also for the loss of the services provided by the deceased. The process of advancing such a claim is governed by the Fatal Accidents Act 1976. Case law then interprets how the statutory law should be applied in certain circumstances. This chapter considers:

a) The legal and factual elements necessary to qualify as a dependant;

b) The statutory definition of a dependant;

c) Criticisms of the current approach.

6.2 QUALIFYING AS A DEPENDANT

For an individual to make a claim for financial loss suffered as a result of another's death they must satisfy the court that they qualify as a dependant. There are two essential elements in the definition of a dependant: one is legal, the other factual. The elements are:

a) Legally the claimant must be a dependant as defined by S1 (3) of the Fatal Accidents Act 1976;

b) As a matter of fact the claimant must be able to demonstrate that they had a reasonable expectation of pecuniary benefit from the deceased.

Both of these elements must be made out or the claim will fail.

Within the broad category of dependants there is a further restricted class of individuals who are entitled to claim the statutory bereavement payment[47] and make a claim for funeral expenses. This category of individuals is separate from the definition of dependants and is a different concept. It is important to note that it is not necessary to prove to the court that there was a reasonable expectation of pecuniary benefit from the deceased when making a claim for funeral expenses or a bereavement award. Claims for funeral expenses and bereavement awards are discussed briefly below in this section on dependency because confusion often arises as to the interaction between these two areas of the statute. For a full discussion of funeral expenses and bereavement awards see chapters fourteen and fifteen respectively.

6.3 THE LEGAL REQUIREMENT – A DEPENDANT ACCORDING TO STATUTE

6.3.1 THE STATUTORY DEFINITION IS STRICT

Unless the Fatal Accidents Act 1976 itself defines the individual as a dependant then they are not a dependant. This is the case even where it can be argued that the application of the test in the Act may result in an outcome that is unfair. In the case of *Swift v Secretary of State for Justice*[48] the Court of Appeal upheld the decision of the High Court that the child of the deceased was entitled to a claim under the Fatal Accidents Act 1976

47 Currently set at £12,980 for deaths that occurred after the 1st of April 2013 and before the 1st May 2020 and at £15,120 after the 1st May 2020.

48 [2013] EWCA Civ 193

but the partner of the deceased and mother to their child was not. This was because the deceased and his partner had not been living together for the necessary two-year period. The court confirmed in this case that this strict interpretation was not incompatible with Articles 14 and 8 of the ECHR.

6.3.2 THE STATUTORY DEFINITION AT S1(3)

The statutory definition of a dependant is crucial. It is set out at sections 1(2) and (3) of the Fatal Accidents Act 1976. It states:

> *(2) Subject to section 1A(2) below, every such action shall be for the benefit of the dependants of the person ("the deceased") whose death has been so caused.*
>
> *(3) In this Act "dependant" means—*
>
> *(a) the wife or husband or former wife or husband of the deceased;*
>
> *(aa) the civil partner or former civil partner of the deceased;*
>
> *(b) any person who—*
>
> *(i) was living with the deceased in the same household immediately before the date of the death; and*
>
> *(ii) had been living with the deceased in the same household for at least two years before that date; and*
>
> *(iii) was living during the whole of that period as the husband or wife or civil partner of the deceased;*
>
> *(c) any parent or other ascendant of the deceased;*
>
> *(d) any person who was treated by the deceased as his parent;*
>
> *(e) any child or other descendant of the deceased;*

(f) any person (not being a child of the deceased) who, in the case of any marriage to which the deceased was at any time a party, was treated by the deceased as a child of the family in relation to that marriage;

(fa) any person (not being a child of the deceased) who, in the case of any civil partnership in which the deceased was at any time a civil partner, was treated by the deceased as a child of the family in relation to that civil partnership;

(g) any person who is, or is the issue of, a brother, sister, uncle or aunt of the deceased.

(4) The reference to the former wife or husband of the deceased in subsection (3)(a) above includes a reference to a person whose marriage to the deceased has been annulled or declared void as well as a person whose marriage to the deceased has been dissolved.

(4A) The reference to the former civil partner of the deceased in subsection (3)(aa) above includes a reference to a person whose civil partnership with the deceased has been annulled as well as a person whose civil partnership with the deceased has been dissolved.

(5) In deducing any relationship for the purposes of subsection (3) above—

(a) any relationship by marriage or civil partnership shall be treated as a relationship by consanguinity, any relationship of the half blood as a relationship of the whole blood, and the stepchild of any person as his child, and

(b) an illegitimate person shall be treated as—

(i) the legitimate child of his mother and reputed father, or

(ii) in the case of a person who has a female parent by virtue of section 43 of the Human Fertilisation and Embryology Act 2008, the legitimate child of his mother and that female parent.

Each class of dependant as defined by S1(3) is discussed in more detail below.

6.3.3 DEPENDANTS ENTITLED TO THE BEREAVEMENT AWARD

It is important to recognise that, although they may overlap, not every dependant listed in S1(3) of the Fatal Accidents Act 1976 is entitled to the stand alone statutory bereavement award. Dependants and those entitled to the bereavement award are two separate and different things. The bereavement award is discussed in more detail at chapter fourteen. The remainder of this chapter will look at the statutory definition of dependants as set out by S1(3) of the Fatal Accidents Act 1976.

6.3.4 SAME-SEX PARTNERSHIPS

The Fatal Accidents Act 1976 was amended by the Civil Partnerships Act 2004[49]. This means that same-sex partners now have the same rights as different-sex couples. Just as with different-sex couples, the surviving partner of a same-sex partnership or marriage is a dependant under the Act if:

a) They were married to the deceased;

b) They were in a civil partnership with the deceased;

c) They were living together for more than two years as civil partners for more than two years before the death of the deceased;

d) They were a former civil partner to the deceased;

49 Civil Partnership Act 2004 (c. 33), ss. 83(7)(a), 263(2); S.I. 2005/3175, art. 2(1), Sch. 1

e) They were a former husband or wife to the deceased.

6.3.5 EX-HUSBANDS AND WIVES AND EX-CIVIL PARTNERS

The definition of husband or wife or civil partner should not cause any practical difficulty. Equally the definition of ex-husband or ex-wife and ex-civil partner is rarely problematic. It is important to remember that the legal status of the ex-spouse or civil partner as a dependant is an absolute one as defined by statute and is not limited by any subsequent remarriage. In the case of *Shepherd v Post Office*[50] the Court rejected the Post Office's contention that Ms Shepherd ceased to become a dependant on her re-marriage[51].

Just because the ex-spouse or ex-civil partner fulfils the first, legal, limb of the test for being a dependant it does not necessarily follow that a successful claim will be made out. The ex-spouse or ex-civil partner must still establish, as a matter of fact, that they had a reasonable expectation of pecuniary benefit from the deceased.

6.3.6 COHABITEES

The Fatal Accidents Act 1976 is clear on how a cohabitee qualifies as a dependant. It states at S1(3)(b) that this is defined as:

(b) any person who—

50 June 15, 1995; Independent, July 31, 1995

51 The Court of Appeal also rejected the argument that, as the claimant had started living with the deceased again following the breakdown of her second marriage she had to "re-qualify" as a dependant by cohabiting with him for two years. She was a dependant by the fact that she was the deceased's ex-wife.

(i) was living with the deceased in the same household immediately before the date of the death; and

(ii) had been living with the deceased in the same household for at least two years before that date; and

(iii) was living during the whole of that period as the husband or wife or civil partner of the deceased;

The statutory definition is strict. Each case is determined on its own facts. In the usual fashion it is for the claimant to prove their case on the balance of probabilities via evidence.

In the case of *Pounder v London Underground Ltd*[52] the couple had a tempestuous relationship and spent periods apart. For part of their relationship the deceased's girlfriend had gone to live in a hostel but had regularly returned home to spend time with the deceased. The court confirmed that there was sufficient evidence to prove that there had been a period of two years of cohabitation as defined by the act and that the "brief absences" did not break this period.

The Court of Appeal case of *Kotke v Saffarini*[53] concerned an appeal from HHJ Hepple QC sitting in Kingston-upon-Hull. The Court of Appeal cited with approval the propositions that HHJ Hepple took from a review of the relevant statutory framework, the case of *Gully v Dix*[54] and the decision in the case of *Pounder*. These were summarised as:

a) Each case was fact sensitive;

b) The relevant word for consideration is "household" not "house";

c) "Living together" is the antithesis of "living apart";

---

52 [1995] PIQR P217

53 [2005] EWCA Civ 221

54 [2004] EWCA Civ 139.

d) The parties may be in the same "household" if they are "tied by their relationship";

e) The "tie" of that relationship may be manifest by many elements, not simply living under one roof but the public and private acknowledgment of their mutual society and the mutual protection and support that binds them together;

HHJ Hepple made the point that "*No factor was necessarily more important than the other or determinative of the issue*".

In that case the Court of Appeal upheld the decision of HHJ Hepple that the claimant did not qualify as a dependant for the purposes of the Fatal Accidents Act 1976 because although they had a child together, they retained separate houses and kept separate households. Although they had expressed a desire to live in the same household this was different from actually doing so.

6.3.7 ANY PARENT OR ASCENDANT OF THE DECEASED

The inclusion of the word "ascendant"[55] means that grandparents and great grandparents fulfil the legal definition of a dependant for the purposes of the Fatal Accidents Act 1976. At the risk of repetition the second, factual, limb of dependency must still be established: that is, the fact that there is a reasonable expectation of pecuniary benefit.

55 The Administration of Justice Act 1982 s3(1) inserted the entitlement for ascendants above the grandparent. Ascendant can be defined in the legal context as: those who from a person is descended; no matter how remote.

6.3.8 ANY PERSON TREATED BY THE DECEASED AS HIS PARENT

There is little useful guidance on this point from reported case law. Although on first impressions the definition put forward by the Act seems a wide one, practically the number of individuals in this position must be very small. As with all proposed dependants, there remains the requirement for the dependant to show that as a matter of fact, there is a reasonable expectation of pecuniary benefit.

6.3.9 ANY CHILD OR OTHER DESCENDANT OF THE DECEASED

Adult children fulfil the legal definition of a dependant. It seems that the law has long recognised that children born after the death of the deceased, but which were in the mother's womb[56] at the time of the deceased's death fulfil the legal definition of a dependant[57]. From 1934 illegitimate children or children by adoption[58] have been recognised as fulfilling the definition of "any child"[59].

The Fatal Accidents Act 1976 specifically sets out how the law is to be applied in relation to illegitimate children and step-children at section 1(5):

> *In deducing any relationship for the purposes of subsection (3) above—*

56 En ventre sa mere

57 The George and the Richard (1871) L.R. 3 A. & E. 466

58 For a definition of how adopted children are treated in law see S39(1) of the Adoption Act 1976

59 These provisions were inserted by the Law Reform (Miscellaneous Provisions) Act 1934.

(a) any relationship by marriage or civil partnership shall be treated as a relationship by consanguinity, any relationship of the half blood as a relationship of the whole blood, and the stepchild of any person as his child, and

(b) an illegitimate person shall be treated as—

(i) the legitimate child of his mother and reputed father, or

(ii) in the case of a person who has a female parent by virtue of section 43 of the Human Fertilisation and Embryology Act 2008, the legitimate child of his mother and that female parent.

The wording "an illegitimate person shall be treated as the legitimate child of his mother" seems straightforward. The inclusion of the wording "a reputed father" suggests that providing the deceased was the "reputed" father of the proposed dependant it does not matter if he was the actual father or not. As far as this author can ascertain this particular area of the Fatal Accidents Act 1976 has not been the subject of clarification in any reported case and it remains to be seen how the Court of Appeal would interpret this area of the statute. It seems obvious that any decision in this area would be fact-sensitive.

6.3.10 ANY PERSON WHO WAS TREATED BY THE DECEASED AS A CHILD OF THE FAMILY IN RELATION TO THAT MARRIAGE OR CIVIL PARTNERSHIP

This wording links the child to the marriage or civil partnership of the deceased. So, if the deceased was in a marriage or civil partnership and within that marriage or civil partnership treated the child as a member of that family, then that child fulfils the legal definition of a dependant. It is suggested that the key word in this part of the statute is "treated". While there is some disagreement among commentators on this issue, this author takes the view that the inclusion of the word "treated" means that the child in question does not have to have been the genetic offspring of either member of the marriage or civil partnership but merely treated as a child in *relation* to that marriage or civil partnership.

This part of the Act as it is currently worded excludes, seemingly unfairly, other children who may, as a matter of fact, have been dependent on the deceased. For example, as it is currently drafted the wording excludes children treated by the deceased as a child of the family if the deceased was not married or in a civil partnership. The unfairness of the wording of this part of S1(3) of the Fatal Accidents Act 1976 and indeed the wording of S1(3) of the Act as a whole, has been identified by a number of commentators and the Law Reform Commission as long ago as 1999. This is discussed in more detail below.

6.3.11 ANY PERSON WHO IS, OR IS THE ISSUE OF, A BROTHER SISTER, UNCLE OR AUNT OF THE DECEASED

This part of the Act covers claims for dependency from brothers, sisters, uncles or aunts of the deceased and also those issuing from the brother, sister, uncle or aunt of the deceased (nieces, nephews, cousins).

6.4 CRITICISMS OF THE STATUTORY DEFINITION OF DEPENDANTS.

For some years now prominent commentators in the area and indeed the Law Reform Commission itself have criticised the current manner in which the Fatal Accidents Act 1976 restricts those who can be a dependant to the list set out at S1(3). The Law Reform Commission, as long ago as 1999, made the point that the restrictive wording of S1(3) of the Act excludes particular classes of persons who they thought "*merited a right of action*"[60]. In particular the Law Reform Commission:

> *highlighted the position of cohabitants who were living together as husband and wife but who do no satisfy the "two year rule"; same-sex couples; children who were not of the deceased but who were supported by the deceased whilst he or she was engaged in a marriage-like relationship with their parent; children otherwise supported by the deceased (such as a friend's children); certain distant relatives supported by the deceased (such as a great nephew supporting a great aunt); and non-relatives who live together but do not enjoy a marriage-like relationship.*

Warming to their theme the Law Reform Commission made the point that:

> *Virtually every consultee to express a view on this matter agreed with our provisional view. The present list was criticised as "arbitrary" and "discriminatory".*

They concluded "*that the list of those who can claim under the Fatal Accidents Act 1976 is too restrictive and should be reformed*" and proposed reforming the list by replacing it with a test "*requiring proof only of the relevant type of loss*".

The Law Commission is correct that a suitably worded statutory test would probably reduce the unfairness caused by the arbitrary nature of the current list whilst creating very little additional complexity in ascertaining who could make a claim. However, a good deal of time has now elapsed since the Law Reform Commission made its recommendations and the current state of the law shows no sign of changing. The case law that has already been discussed in relation to

60 Law Commission Report No 263 Claims for Wrongful Death paragraph 3.16

S1(3) makes it very clear that unless an individual falls within the statutory definition of a dependant as set out at S1(3), a claim will fail.

6.5 THE FACTUAL REQUIREMENT – A REASONABLE EXPECTATION OF PECUNIARY LOSS

For an individual to qualify as a dependant for the purposes of an action under Fatal Accidents Act 1976 they must not only satisfy the court that they are a dependant as defined by statute, but they must also show that, as a matter of fact, they had a "reasonable expectation of pecuniary benefit"[61].

It has been clear since at least the case of *Franklin*[62] that it is not necessary for the dependant to prove that the deceased was under a legal liability to support him or her. However, where a claim is made by a common law spouse or civil partner section 3(4) of the Act requires the court to take into account the fact that there is no legal liability to provide for the surviving partner when determining the amount of damages to be awarded. Section 3(4) states:

> *In an action under this Act where there fall to be assessed damages payable to a person who is a dependant by virtue of section 1(3)(b) above in respect of the death of the person with whom the dependant was living as husband or wife or civil partner there shall be taken into account (together with any other matter that appears to the court to be relevant to the action) the fact that the dependant had no enforceable right to financial support by the deceased as a result of their living together.*

61 Franklin v South Eastern Railway (1858) 3 H.&N. 211

62 Ibid

In the case of *Drew v Abassi*[63] the Court of Appeal upheld a decision where the trial judge reduced the multiplier from 15 to 13 to take account of the fact that the dependant in question was not married but was a common law spouse. There are some commentators who make the point that the requirement for the court to take this into account only with common law spouses and civil partners does not appear fair.

There is no need for the dependant to show that at the time of the death he or she was actually receiving a pecuniary benefit. It is sufficient to show that there was a reasonable expectation of a pecuniary benefit in the future[64].

The phrase "reasonable expectation" means that the dependant is effectively making a claim for a loss of a chance. As such, it is not necessary for the dependant to prove on a balance of probabilities that he actually would have been in receipt of a pecuniary benefit in the future. The test is more forgiving than that. The dependant must prove that there was a *substantial chance* of receiving a pecuniary benefit. If the chance is substantial the court must evaluate that chance.

In the case of *Davies v Taylor*[65] the House of Lords stated:

> *To obtain anything under a head of substantial losses of future chance, the plaintiff must establish that that chance was substantial. If it was, it must be evaluated. If it was a mere possibility, it must be ignored. Many different words could be and have been used to indicate the dividing line. I can think of none better than 'substantial', on the one hand, or 'speculative' on the other. It must be left to the good sense of the tribunal to decide on broad lines,*

63 (Unreported, CA, 24 May 1995)

64 See the case of Franklin, op cit, where the point was made that in the future a parent may require assistance and see Taff Vale Railway v Jenkins [1913] A.C. 1 where an argument was made that a child may provide financial assistance in the future.

65 [1974] AC 207

> *without regard to legal niceties, but on a consideration of all the facts in proper perspective.*

The types of pecuniary loss that give rise to a valid claim under the Fatal Accidents Act 1976 are discussed in detail in chapter eight.

6.6 SUMMARY

In summary:

a) A dependant must fulfil the statutory definition of a dependant as set out at S1(3) of the Fatal Accidents Act 1976;

b) In addition, a dependant must also satisfy the court that, as a matter of fact, they had a reasonable expectation of pecuniary benefit from the deceased;

c) It is not necessary to prove that there was a legal requirement to support the dependant;

d) If the dependant is a common law spouse or civil partner then section 3(4) of the Fatal Accidents Act 1976 requires the court to take into account the fact that there is no legal liability to provide for the surviving partner when determining the amount of damages to be awarded. This can affect the amount of damages that are awarded;

e) The dependant does not need to show that they were receiving a pecuniary benefit at the time of death. An expectation of receiving one in the future is sufficient;

f) It is not necessary for the dependant to prove on a balance of probabilities that he actually would have been in receipt of a pecuniary benefit;

g) The dependant must prove that there was a *substantial chance* of receiving a pecuniary benefit.

CHAPTER SEVEN

THE CALCULATION OF CLAIMS FOR DEPENDENCY

7.1 INTRODUCTION

In this chapter the calculation of claims for dependency is looked at in detail. The matters which must be excluded from any calculations are discussed. The main types of dependency claim and their calculation are covered in detail. More unusual dependency claims are looked at and the calculation of damages in these claims is discussed in detail.

7.2 MATTERS WHICH MUST BE EXCLUDED FROM DEPENDENCY CLAIMS

When advancing a claim for dependency, benefits arising from death are excluded from the calculation of damages. Benefits to widows or widowers from remarriage are similarly excluded, as are any benefits to child dependants that may arise from new marriages or new family arrangements. In some ways this is counter to the normal rules of tortious compensation. This chapter considers in more detail the exclusion of benefits arising from death.

7.2.1 BENEFITS ARISING FROM DEATH

The death of an individual can give rise to financial benefits in the form of insurance payments, pension payments and the like. It can also give rise to new family arrangements as widows and widowers remarry and enter into new relationships. These new family arrangements can, in turn, benefit the dependants of the deceased.

The current position is that all benefits arising from death are excluded when calculating damages for dependency.

This was not always the case. Historically the law took into account benefits that had occurred because of death when calculating damages for dependency claims. This meant that the court would take into account such matters as insurance policies, pensions and new family arrangements that had arisen because of the death when calculating the damages that flowed from the death[66]. Over the first half of the twentieth century this position was completely changed as amendments were made to the law[67].

These amendments ultimately resulted in section 2 of the Fatal Accidents Act 1959 where a list of the benefits that were to be ignored was set out. Following recommendations from the Law Commission and the Royal Commission on Civil Liability and Compensation for Personal Injury, the list approach was then replaced by the broadly worded test which is currently set out at section 4 of the Fatal Accidents Act 1976[68].

Section 4 of the Fatal Accidents Act 1976 now states:

> *In assessing damages in respect of a person's death under this Act, benefits which have accrued or will or may accrue to any person from his estate or otherwise as a result of his death shall be disregarded.*

66 See the speech of Lord Macmillan at para 609 in the case of Davies v Powell Duffryn Collieries [1942] A.C. 601

67 See the amendments made by the Fatal Accidents (Damages) Act 1908, the Widows', Orphans' and Old Age Contributory Pensions Act 1929 and the Law Reform (Personal Injuries) Act 1948 respectively.

68 Report on Personal Injury Litigation – Assessment of Damages (1973) Law Com No 56 paras 254-356; Royal Commission on Civil Liability and Compensation for Personal Injury 1978 Cmnd 7054-I paras 537-539.

The Court of Appeal has expressly confirmed that the old second stage in the calculation of damages (where any benefits the dependant had received as a result of the death were deducted from the damages awarded) has now been "swept away"[69] by section 4.

It is important to appreciate the impact that the broad nature of this test has on the calculation of claims for dependency. The inclusion of the words "or otherwise" means that the matters which are to be disregarded are much broader than those envisaged by previous versions of the Fatal Accidents Act.

The broad nature of the test can give rise to situations where the amount of damages received exceeds the sum necessary to place the dependent back in the financial position they enjoyed before the deceased's death. As far back as 1979 Lord Diplock expressed concerns that:

> *...the assessment of damages in fatal accident cases has become an artificial and conjectural exercise. Its purpose is no longer to put dependants, particularly widows, into the same economic position as they would have been had their late husband lived.*[70]

Criticism of the open ended nature of the test at section 4 continues to this day. The latest Law Commission report has recommended a return to the list based approach because of concerns that section 4 suffers from "overinclusiveness"[71] and is difficult to interpret. However, for present purposes, the broadly worded test at section 4 is the starting point for matters which must be excluded when approaching the calculation of any dependency claim under the Fatal Accidents Act 1976.

69 Arnup v M.W. White Ltd [2008] I.C.R. 1064 CA

70 Cookson v Knowles [1979] A.C 556

71 The Law Commission (Law Com No 263) Claims for Wrongful Death para 5.21

7.2.2 INSURANCE POLICIES, WORK SCHEME PAYOUTS AND PENSIONS

These are all benefits that arise from death. They are all excluded, entirely, from the calculation of dependency in a claim under the Fatal Accidents Act 1976. The Court of Appeal confirmed that this is the correct approach in the recent case of *Arnup v M.W. White Ltd*[72].

In this case the widow of the deceased had received two sums of money from the defendant's "death in service benefit scheme" and an employee benefit trust. The defendant argued that these sums should be taken into account when calculating the widow's financial dependency under the Fatal Accidents Act 1976. The Court of Appeal, reversing the judgment at first instance, stated that section 4 operated so that "all benefits which came to the widow as a result of the death are to be disregarded"[73].

7.2.3 REMARRIAGE

Under the Fatal Accidents Act 1976, any benefits from re-marriage are excluded from the calculation of dependency claims, and this is the case for widows or widowers who remarry. However, section 3(3) of the Act specifically sets out an exception in relation to a wife's remarriage. It states:

> *a) In an action under this Act where there fall to be assessed damages payable to a widow in respect of the death of her husband there shall not be taken account the re-marriage of the widow or her prospects of re-marriage.*

The wording of section 3 (3) appears unfair because it relates solely to widows and their prospect of remarriage but does not relate to widowers.

---

72 [2008] I.C.R 1064 CA

73 Ibid para 26

However, the broad wording of section 4 makes it clear that if a widower remarries the benefit from this new marriage must also be ignored when calculating any dependency claim[74].

7.2.4 NEW FAMILY ARRANGEMENTS

Remarriage or new family arrangements will often have a (positive) impact on services that are provided for a child. This impact is ignored when calculating dependency claims. A child dependant can still claim for the loss of financial dependency and services provided by a deceased parent even when a new family arrangement means that, in fact, the care provided is now "better" than that provided by the deceased parent. The wording of section 4 clearly covers these circumstances.

That section 4 operates in this manner was expressly confirmed in the case of *Stanley v Saddique*[75]. The decision in this case confirms that both a widower's remarriage and the benefits from new family arrangements are excluded from the calculation of dependency claims.

In this case the issue was the loss of the mother's services. The father had re-married and the judge at first instance had determined that his new wife was providing better services as a mother than the deceased. The issue of whether the use of the word "widow" in section 3 (3) meant that bencfits to widowers remarrying should be included in the calculations was examined on appeal. The Court of Appeal confirmed that if a widower remarries the benefits of that are to be ignored in the same way as at a widow's remarriage. Purchas LJ observed:

> *...section 3(3) was left in as being a particularly significant question of policy but that by section 4 Parliament intended to further the*

74 Section 3(3) is now otiose. It is another example of how the law in this area has developed in a piece meal and uncoordinated fashion.

75 [1991] 2 WLR 459

> *departure from ordinary common law assessment of damages for personal injuries by the artificial concept which has for many decades been the basis of damages recoverable under the Fatal Accidents Acts.*

The fact that any benefits to the child dependant flowing from the new family arrangement were to be excluded from the calculation of the dependency damages was also confirmed. Purchas LJ went on to state:

> *For the reasons I have just given I have come to the conclusion that the judge was correct in his decision that the benefits accruing to the minor as a result of his absorption into the family unit consisting of his father and stepmother and siblings should be wholly disregarded for the purposes of assessing damages.*

The approach in *Stanley* has been followed and applied in the cases of *R v Criminal Injuries Compensation Board Ex p. K*[76], *L (A Child) v Barry May Haulage*[77] and *H v S*[78]. In all of these cases it was held that the new support services provided to the children following the death of their parent is a benefit resulting from death that must be disregarded when calculating dependency.

There are cases where the courts have misapplied the principle in section 4. At first instance in the case of *Watson v Willmott*[79] damages were reduced because the child had been adopted by his aunt and uncle. In the case of *Hayden v Hayden*[80] the Court of Appeal declined to follow the reasoning in *Stanley v Saddique* and took into account the benefit to the child claimant of the services of his father which were taking the place of those of the child's deceased mother. Given the clear wording of section

76 [1999] QB 1131

77 [2002] P.I.Q.R Q5 pg35

78 [2003] Q.B. 965 CA

79 [1991] 1 Q.B. 140

80 [1992] 1 W.L.R. 986

4 and the equally clear decision in the case of *Arnup* this author is not alone in considering that these cases were wrongly decided.

7.2.5 THE CASE OF STEVE HILL LTD v WITHAM

At first blush the case of *Steve Hill Ltd v Witham*[81] may seem to be a case where the Court of Appeal considered a new family arrangement when assessing the level of dependency. This is not so. In *Steve Hill Ltd*, the Court of Appeal found that new factual circumstances had arisen since the initial trial which meant that the factual basis for the dependency claim no longer existed. Accordingly, the matter was remitted to the trial Judge to re-evaluate the nature and extent of any dependency. The facts of the case are unusual.

Mr Witham had died from mesothelioma caused by exposure to asbestos when working for Steve Hill Ltd. Mr and Mrs Witham had fostered two children on permanent placements. They had decided that Mrs Witham would return to full-time work as a specialist nurse and that Mr Witham would be the parent at home. The couple received a fostering allowance. Mrs Witham continued to receive the allowance after her husband's death but stopped work to look after the children.

Mrs Witham brought a claim as a dependant. At first instance the Judge found that the relevant dependency was Mrs Witham's, not the children's. He stated that Mrs Witham had depended on Mr Witham to look after the children, so that she could pursue her career. The judge held that replacement care at commercial rates was the appropriate measure of loss.

81 [2021] EWCA Civ 1312

Between the initial trial and the appeal, the foster children were not returned to Mrs Witham's care following a period of respite care[82].

The Court of Appeal found that: *"It is the unforeseen and undisputed fact that the children have been removed from Mrs Witham. It follows that since their removal the factual basis of the dependency claim no longer exists."*[83] Applying the principles in *Ladd v Marshall*[84] the Court of Appeal admitted the new factual basis in as evidence and stated that *"…the only reasonable course is to remit this matter to the trial judge to allow for a re-evaluation of the claimant's dependency in the light of the new evidence."*[85]

7.3 BUSINESS RELATIONSHIPS

Sometimes the deceased will have been in a business relationship with the claimant as well as a family relationship. A common example of this is a father and son or husband and wife business. In this situation losses related to business loss are excluded when calculating damages in a dependency claim.

The origin of this rule can be traced to the case of *Burgess v Florence Nightingale Hospital for Gentlewomen*[86]. In that case husband and wife were professional dancing partners. The husband's earning capacity decreased following his wife's death and as part of his claim he advanced a claim for this loss. It was held that in order to be recoverable under the Fatal Accidents Act the benefit must be *"a benefit which arises from the relationship between the parties"*[87]. The husband's claim for his loss of

---

82 Ibid, paras 21-25

83 Ibid, para 29

84 [1954] 1 WLR 1489

85 Steve Hill Ltd v Witham [2021] EWCA Civ 1312, para 34

86 [1955] 1 Q.B. 349

87 Ibid at 354

earnings from the dancing business failed. Devlin J stated that *"there was no benefit arising in the dancing partnership that can be properly attributed to the relationship of husband and wife"*[88].

The principle in *Burgess* has been considered and applied in the case of *Cox v Hockenhull*[89]. In that case part of the claim that was advanced was for the loss of the care allowance that the claimant had received for caring for the deceased. The Court of Appeal (reversing the decision at first instance on this aspect of the case) stated that the loss of the invalid care allowance was not recoverable. Stuart Smith LJ stated:

> *"In effect the state employed Mr Cox to care for a severely disabled person. If that person had been anyone other than his wife, the fact that she died and Mr Cox thereby lost his income, would not give rise to compensatable loss. The fact that the relationship of marriage existed is as Devlin J. put it 'incidental'."*[90]

It is sometimes difficult to determine where the dividing line between a loss arising from a business relationship and a loss arising from a relationship of dependency falls.

In the case of *Malyon v Plummer*[91] the deceased had paid his wife a generous salary for her contribution to the family business. The salaries of both the husband and the wife were paid into the husband's account and then the family expenses were covered from that account. The claimant stated that the entire amount that she and her children received from the account should form the basis of the dependency calculation. The defendant stated that the amount that was from the wife's salary should be deducted because this arose from a business relationship as in the case of *Burgess* and not from a relationship of husband and wife. The

88 Ibid at 361

89 [2000] 1 W.L.R 750 CA

90 Ibid at para 18

91 [1964] 1 Q.B. 330 CA

court rejected the defendant's argument on the basis that it was *"unconvincing"* to state that the wife had lost her salary as the result of being deprived of her co-director. The court instead found that the cause of the loss was *"that she has lost her husband who was the family bread winner"*[92].

In the case of *Welsh Ambulance Services NHS Trust v Williams*[93] the deceased had brought family members into his successful business. The defendant attempted to argue (albeit only at the appeal stage) that this loss was a business loss and as such not recoverable. The Court of Appeal disagreed on the basis that the real substance of this relationship was one of a family relationship not a business relationship. Concluding the appeal Smith LJ summarised the law in this area:

> "...*Burgess v Florence Hospital for Gentlewomen [1955] 1 QB 349 [...] is authority for the proposition that where the relationship between the claimant and the deceased was primarily a business relationship, the claimant cannot claim a dependency merely because he or she also happens to fall within the class of dependants of the deceased. The Fatal Accidents Act does not give a right of recovery for the loss of business profits by the surviving business partner(s) on the death of one partner. It provides a right of recovery for the loss of a dependency which is founded in the relationship of husband and wife (or parent and child or whatever the relationship was). If the relationship was primarily that of business partners, the mere fact that the partners happen to be husband and wife or father and son does not enable the survivor to claim a dependency on the death of the other partner. If the relationship is primarily that of a family, it matters not that their financial arrangements take the form of a*

92 Ibid at 345-346

93 [2008] EWCA Civ 81

business partnership. [...] The court will look at the substance of the relationship and the real nature of the support provided."[94]

The issue of business losses was considered in the relatively recent Court of Appeal case of *Paramount Shopfitting Co Ltd v Rix*[95], Nicola Davis LJ summarised the key principles the Court must adopt when assessing damages to be awarded:

i) The question to be addressed is what is the extent of the dependants' loss based upon a reasonable expectation of pecuniary benefit from the continuance of the life of the deceased;

ii) The assessment is dependent upon the facts of the particular case;

iii) Capital assets which the dependants had the benefit of during the deceased's lifetime and continued to enjoy following the death are not taken into account either as part of the dependency or as a deduction from it;

iv) The question for the court is how much loss has arisen because the deceased is no longer alive and able to work, and how much of the deceased's income was derived solely from capital which the dependants have inherited;

v) The dependency is fixed at the moment of death, it is what the dependants would probably have received as benefit from the deceased had the deceased lived. Post death events are irrelevant, save for those which affect the continuance of the dependency and the rise or fall in earnings to reflect the effects of inflation;

vi) The damages awarded under the FAA can be greater than would be justified upon a strict view of the dependants' loss."

94 Ibid at para 52

95 [2021] EWCA Civ 1172 at para 54.

In the case of *Paramount* the Court considered the issue of capital assets. Mr Rix died from Mesothelioma in 2016. His Mesothelioma was caused by the Defendant company. After leaving his role with the defendant Mr Rix established a successful joinery business. He owned 40% of the shares in the company. His two sons both worked for the business, and each had 10% shareholdings. His widow owned the remaining 40% of the shares and was also a director. She was in receipt of both a director's salary and dividend income from her shares, as was the deceased. However, Mrs Rix had no active involvement in the business. Her position as a director and shareholder was for tax reasons. After Mr Rix died, she inherited her husband's shares, giving her an 80% shareholding. One of the sons took over as managing director and other managers were also appointed to run the business. The company continued to thrive, with turnover and profits increasing in each year after the death. Arguably, Mrs Rix's personal financial position was improved following Mr Rix's death[96].

At first instance the High Court found that Mr Rix was the prime mover within the business and that his widow was dependent on the income he derived from his work in the business. Cavanagh J determined that all the director's fees and dividends (paid to both the deceased and his wife) had came from income made by Mr Rix's labour.

At appeal the Defendant sought to argue that the share in the business Mrs Rix had inherited was a capital asset[97]. They argued that the business "continued to have a substantial value and income producing capacity"[98] even without Mr Rix's involvement. The Defendant submitted that the damages awarded for dependency should be

96 She had an 80% share in the business as opposed to 40. The business had grown since the death and was likely to continue to do so.

97 Three grounds of appeal were advanced, see paras 42-48. For the purposes of this chapter only the first ground is discussed.

98 Ibid at para 44

reduced and quantified with reference to the cost of employing someone else to do Mr Rix's job so that the income from Mr Rix's work could be clearly separated from the income derived from the capital asset (the business).

The Court of Appeal rejected the Defendant's arguments. Giving the leading judgment Nicola Davis LJ offered the following definition of a capital asset:

> *"Income is only derived from capital if it is identifiable as having been received without the labour and services of the deceased. In short, it is passive. On the facts of this case, there was no identifiable element of the profits which was not touched by the management of Mr Rix."*

While not establishing any new law, the case of Rix is a timely reminder that:

a) When looking at business relationships a key issue for the Court will be whether there was passive income from the business that will be unaffected by the loss of the deceased;

b) Each case is highly fact sensitive;

c) Damages in relation to dependency can be greater than the actual financial loss sustained[99].

7.4 SUMMARY

In summary:

99 See para 39 where the case of Arnup v MW White Ltd [2008] EWCA Civ 447 is cited with approval: "That is what Parliament has decided and the fact that the claimant will in many cases receive more than she has lost is nothing to the point."

a) When advancing a claim for dependency, benefits arising from death are excluded from the calculation of damages;

b) Any benefits from re-marriage are excluded from the calculation of dependency claims, and this is the case for widows or widowers who remarry;

c) Any benefits that flow from new family arrangements post death are excluded from the calculation of dependency claims;

d) Losses related to business loss are excluded when calculating damages in a dependency claim;

e) A key consideration when examining business losses is ascertaining what part of the businesses income derived from "passive income";

f) Each case is fact sensitive;

g) The correct application of the law can result in a situation where the damages awarded can be greater than the financial loss sustained.

CHAPTER EIGHT

GENERAL PRINCIPLES IN CALCULATING A DEPENDENCY CLAIM

8.1 INTRODUCTION

A claim for dependency is a claim for the loss of the pecuniary benefit arising from the relationship that the dependant had with the deceased. This pecuniary benefit can be in the form of money or services or both.

Claims for bereavement, funeral expenses, the pain suffering and loss of amenity of the deceased and other losses of the deceased are not part of a dependency claim but can form the subject of other claims under the Fatal Accidents Act 1976 and the Law Reform (Miscellaneous Provisions) Act 1934. These other types of claim are discussed at chapters fourteen, fifteen and sixteen respectively.

8.2 THE MATHEMATICAL APPROACH

The general approach to calculating dependency is by a multiplicand and multiplier process. The multiplicand is the present annual value of the dependency. This figure is based on the deceased's income and the services the deceased provided to the dependants. An adjustment is made to this figure to deduct the portion of income and services which solely benefitted the deceased.

The multiplier is a figure which is based on the amount of time in years that the dependency is likely to continue for. This figure is then reduced to account for the fact that the claimant will be receiving the damages as one lump sum. The multiplier can also be reduced to account for other contingencies. The multiplier and the multiplicand are multiplied together to arrive at a final figure of damages. Where necessary and appropriate, a number of different multipliers can be used.

Lord Wright summarised the process in the case of *Davies v Powell Duffryn Associated Collieries Ltd*[100] when he stated:

> *The starting point is the amount of wages which the deceased was earning, the ascertainment of which to some extent may depend on the regularity of his employment. Then there is an estimate of how much was required or expended for his own personal and living expenses. The balance will give a datum or basic figure* [now referred to as the "multiplicand"] *which will generally be turned into a lump sum by taking a certain number of years' purchase* [the "multiplier"].

The calculations that the court make to arrive at the correct multiplicand and multiplier are discussed in more detail below.

8.3 DEPARTURES FROM THE MATHEMATICAL APPROACH

Although the courts primarily adopt a mathematical "multiplier and multiplicand" approach, awards in fatal accident cases have their origin in jury awards and accordingly mathematical calculations are not the only consideration for the court.

In the relatively rare instances where mathematical calculations return a result which is obviously at odds with the facts of the case, the court is not bound to blindly follow the mathematical approach. In the case of *Daniels v Jones*[101] Holyroyd Pearce LJ stated:

100 [1942] A.C. 601 at 617

101 [1961] 1 WLR 1103

> *It must be remembered that this is a question of fact expressly left to the jury ... Since the question is one of actual material loss, some arithmetical calculations are necessary. But they do not provide a substitute for common sense. Much of the calculation could be in the realms of hypothesis, and in that region arithmetic is a good servant but a bad master.*

Awards for dependency are particularly fact sensitive. In the case of *Wood v Bentall Simplex Ltd* Bedlam LJ stated: *"No aspect of the law of damages has been found in practice to be more dependent upon the facts of each particular case that the assessment of loss of pecuniary benefit to dependants under the Fatal Accidents Act"*[102]. Sometimes the particular facts of the case merit a complete departure from the mathematical approach.

In practice the mathematical approach is usually only completely departed from when there is insufficient evidence on which to base an accurate calculation or when there are too many uncertain factors in a case. The case of *Stanley v Saddique*[103] is an example of this. In this case the deceased's employment record consisted of sporadic and poorly paid work and the trial judge concluded that an award made on the traditional multiplicand and multiplier approach was impossible. Instead, the judge awarded a round sum of £5,000 for loss of financial support. The trial judge did award a sum of £24,000 for loss of services as a mother on a multiplier and multiplicand approach. This award was overturned by the Court of Appeal who substituted a lower award of £10,000 which was arrived at "on a jury award basis"[104] not on a multiplier and multiplicand basis.

102 *Wood v Bentall Simplex Ltd [1992] PIQR p332* at para 342

103 [1992] Q.B. 1 CA

104 Per Purchas L.J Ibid at 16C

8.4 CALCULATING THE MULTIPLICAND

The multiplicand is the annual amount in pounds and pence that the deceased provided to the dependant. The starting point in calculating the multiplicand is usually the amount earned by the deceased. The multiplicand is also made up of any other matters of value which the deceased provided to the dependant(s) such as gifts, holidays, etc.

In addition, the services the deceased provided to the dependant(s) are given an annual financial value and this is included in the multiplicand. In instances where the deceased did not work but was, for example, a mother who provided child care services then the value of the services provided by the deceased will be the starting point. Each area involved in calculating the multiplicand is discussed in detail below.

8.4.1 THE DECEASED'S EARNING CAPACITY

The starting point when calculating the amount of money earned by the deceased is usually the annual salary the deceased was earning at the time of death. In common with other personal injury claims earnings are calculated after deductions for tax and national insurance[105].

In addition to the salary itself, other benefits from the employment should be taken into account. The loss of benefits such as a company car are clearly recoverable in a loss of dependency claim[106]. The court will not award the full value of the car, as part of its use will have been for the deceased. The proportion of the car's use that was for the benefit of the family is taken into account along with other factors such as depreciation and running costs.

105 British Transport Commission v Gourley [1956] A.C. 185

106 Clay v Pooler [1982] 3 All ER 570

Careful thought should also be given to any other benefits that the employment conferred, such as any discounts provided by the deceased's employer on goods or any access to cheaper or free health care. It has long been established that the value of goods the deceased brought into the home are included in the calculations for loss of dependency[107].

In particular careful consideration should be given to future pension provision of the deceased as this is also recoverable in a dependency claim[108]. Often the calculations involved in working out the likely value of the pension on retirement are complex and may merit the appointment of an independent expert.

8.4.2 LIKELY CHANGE IN EARNINGS

The court will take into account the fact that the deceased's wage would have been likely to rise or fall in the future. If the deceased's employment was sporadic or temporary the defendant may advance an argument that, had they lived, in the future the deceased would have earned less than at the time of death. A relatively common argument for the claimant is that the deceased was likely to receive a promotion in the future and thus earn more.

In the case of *Young v Percival*[109] the evidence showed that the deceased, who was a salesman at the time of his death, was likely to receive a series of promotions over the course of his career. The court accepted that the promotions were likely and took the likely increase of wages into account when calculating the amount of the dependency.

107 Dalton v South Eastern Railway Company (1858) 4 CB (NS) 296

108 Feay v Barnwell [1938] 1 All ER 31

109 [1975] 1 W.L.R. 17

In the case of *Dalzeil v Donald*[110] the defendant argued that because of the deceased's poor army record he would not have been promoted and might actually have been discharged from the army. The Court of Appeal rejected this argument, preferring the evidence called by the claimant on the point, and found that despite the deceased's disciplinary issues there was a substantial chance of promotion.

The court can deal with likely increases or decreases in the deceased's wage by either altering the multiplicand; using two or more multiplicands for different periods of dependency; or by altering the multiplier used. In the case of *Mallett v McMonagle*[111] Lord Diplock stated that:

> *...anticipated future variations in "dependency" are normally dealt with by adjustment in the multiplicand.*

An increased multiplicand was used in *Robertson v Lestrange*[112], as also were two different multiplicands: one for the years when the children were dependent and another for the years where solely the widow would be dependent.

8.4.3 STATE BENEFITS

If the deceased received state benefits these can be included in the loss of earning capacity calculation. This principle was confirmed in the case of *Cox v Hockenhull*[113] where the deceased was in receipt of disability benefits and some income support. Stuart-Smith LJ stated:

110 [2001] PIQR Q44

111 [1970] A.C. 166

112 [1985] 1 All E.R. 950

113 [2000] 1 W.L.R 750 CA

> *If there is a loss, it cannot matter that the source of income both before and after death is the state, whether as employer or provider of state benefits. I cannot see that the fact that the benefits are all non-contributory makes any difference.*[114]

The case of *Cox* makes it clear that when including state benefits in a claim for dependency the key question for the court is whether there has been a loss caused by the death. Not all state benefits will be lost following the death of an individual and care needs to be taken to examine the difference in the position before and after death. In the case of *Cox* there was no recovery for housing benefit and council tax benefit because as these continued after the death; there was no loss.

8.4.4 DEATH OF A BUSINESSMAN

In cases where the deceased earned a fixed salary, calculating the value of the annual multiplicand is relatively straightforward. However, where the deceased was a self-employed businessman, an individual who lived off investing capital for return, or similar, the calculations involved in working out the likely loss of earning capacity are often more complex. The level of earnings may vary, the level of taxation on the earnings is often more complex and the likely level of any savings that the deceased would have made throughout his life (and then left to his dependants) needs to be taken into account. Each case will turn on its own facts, and the court will make a detailed inquiry into each relevant factor. A good example of the type of detailed consideration the court undertakes in such a case can be found in the case of *Daniels v Jones*[115].

114 Ibid at para 13

115 [1961] 1 W.L.R. 1103 CA

8.4.5 DEATH OF A BUSINESSMAN WHERE THE BUSINESS CONTINUES AFTER DEATH, LIVING OFF CAPITAL

Arguments are often advanced by the defendant that because the business survives the deceased and continues to generate revenue the dependants have not suffered any financial loss. This argument rarely succeeds. The approach by the courts is to examine the facts of each case and ascertain whether a loss has occurred.

In the case of *Wood v Bentall Simplex Ltd*[116] the deceased was a farmer. He was in partnership with his brother and parents and held a third interest in the business. The defendant contended that the widow and children had suffered no loss of dependency because the widow had inherited the third share in the farming business and the business continued to generate income. The court determined that because the income received before the deceased's death resulted primarily from his work on the farm, as opposed to the capital invested in the farm, a loss of dependency to a certain extent had been made out.

The case of *Cape Distribution v O'Loughlin*[117] deals with the situation where the business is less successful after the deceased's death. In *Cape* the deceased made his living from property development. His widow inherited the property portfolio on his death. The widow had not been involved in the business before the deceased's death. Afterwards she attempted to manage the portfolio for a while without success. The Court of Appeal found that a loss of dependency was made out in the form of the loss of the deceased's skill as a manager of the property portfolio. The dependency was valued as the cost of replacing the deceased's skills as a manager.

116 [1992] P.I.Q.R. P332 CA

117 [2001] P.I.Q.R. Q8 CA

The case of *Welsh Ambulance Services NHS Trust v Williams*[118] deals with the situation where the business is more successful after the deceased's death. In this case the deceased was an entrepreneur who had built up a successful business which employed his wife and his two oldest children. On the deceased's death the business was split equally between the family members. The business skills of the children made the business more successful than it had been at the time the deceased was alive. Arguably the dependants were in a better financial position than when the deceased was alive. The court stated that this made no difference to the claim for dependency as this was fixed at the moment of death[119]. A loss of dependency was established and was calculated as the cost of replacing the deceased's business skills.

In the case of *Paramount Shopfitting Co Ltd v Rix* Lady Justice Nicola Davies summarised the principles in this area:

> *"Capital assets which the dependants had the benefit of during the deceased's lifetime and continued to enjoy following the death are not taken into account either as part of the dependency or as a deduction from it;*
>
> *The question for the court is how much loss has arisen because the deceased is no longer alive and able to work, and how much of the deceased's income was derived solely from capital which the dependants have inherited..."*[120]

118 [2008] EWCA Civ 81 CA

119 *Welsh Ambulance* remains the leading authority on this principle. For a more recent example of how this principle operates see: *Paramount Shopfitting Co Ltd v Rix [2021] EWCA Civ 1172.*

120 Paramount Shopfitting Co Ltd v Rix [2021] EWCA Civ 1172 at para 54.

8.4.6 GIFTS, HOLIDAYS, LUXURIES ETC.

A claim can also be advanced for the loss of holidays, gifts and luxuries provided by the deceased. This type of claim is common where the claim is being made by a dependant child who has lost a parent. This type of claim needs to be carefully evidenced in witness statements given that often there is a lack of documentary evidence.

In the case of *Betney v Rowland and Mallard*[121] three daughters had lost their parents in an accident. Their claims for the cost of the likely contributions their parents would have made to their weddings succeeded.

8.5 LOSS OF SERVICES

In addition to the loss of income, a loss of dependency claim includes the cost of replacing the services the deceased provided to the dependants. In cases where the deceased was not the family "breadwinner" but provided childcare this can often form the majority of the multiplicand and special considerations apply.

8.5.1 SERVICES OTHER THAN CHILDCARE

Claims can be made for loss of services that the deceased provided free of charge such as (but not limited to) DIY services and gardening. The case of *Crabtree v Wilson*[122] is an example of a case where the court awarded damages for the value of the deceased's work around the home. In that case the court determined that the annual value of those services was £1,500.

121 [1992] CLY 1786

122 [1993] PIQR Q24

As previously discussed, in the cases of *Cape*[123] and *Williams*[124] the approach of the court in valuing the replacement of services is to value the lost services by reference to the cost of replacing them with professional services. The same principle applies to the replacement of gardening or DIY services. In principle an award can be made for the loss of these services even though up to the date of the trial no replacement services have been purchased (see the fuller discussion of the case of *Knauer v Ministry of Justice*[125] at chapter ten).

8.5.2 LOSS OF THE SERVICES OF A PARENT OR CARER

This is often the main head of loss under loss of services and can frequently be relatively substantial. It is a head of loss that is long established. In the case of *Berry v Humm*[126] it was held that the claims under the Fatal Accidents Act permitted the recovery of damages to replace the loss of services rendered to the household and were not restricted simply to claims for the loss of money or goods. The death of a carer can also give rise to a claim for loss of services[127].

The starting point for calculating the cost of replacing the services is the net cost of replacing the services by hiring a professional housekeeper, nanny, cook, etc.[128]. Such claims can also include the cost of board and lodging for the housekeeper[129]. The cost is still recoverable where the

123 Cape Distribution v O'Loughlin [2001] PIQR Q8

124 Welsh Ambulance Services v Williams [2008] EWCA Civ 71

125 Knauer v Ministry of Justice [2014] EWHC 2553 (QB)

126 [1915] 1 K.B. 627

127 Thomas v Kwik Save Stores Ltd, The Times, June 27, 2000 CA

128 Corbett v Barking Havering and Brentwood Health Authority [1991] 2 Q.B. 408 CA

129 Jeffrey v Smith [1970] R.T.R 279 CA

housekeeper is a relative[130]. The court uses these figures as guidance when assessing the likely value of the loss. It is not the case that the court will simply adopt the figures; careful consideration is given to the facts of the case and the court attempts to make a realistic award. As the children grow older and become more independent courts recognise that the level of dependency on parental care diminishes and calculations need to take this into account[131].

Defendants often argue that awarding the full commercial cost of replacing childcare services overvalues this head of loss. In the case of *Steve Hill Ltd v Witham*[132] the Claimant had taken over childcare duties following her husband's death. The Defendant argued that applying the full commercial rate was inappropriate given the savings the Claimant would make including not paying tax or national insurance charges. Lady Justice Nicola Davies rejected this argument:

> *"In assessing the measure of the loss, the words of Latham LJ at [11] of O'Loughlin are relevant, namely that there is no "prescriptive method by which such damage is to be identified, or calculated ...". What the claimant has lost is the benefit of the service which her husband provided in caring for the children. That being so, she can legitimately claim the cost of securing those services to enable her to place herself in the position she was prior to her husband's death. The value of his service is not affected by the fact that the claimant is required to care for the children pursuant to the fostering arrangements."*[133]

At the risk of repetition, it is important to remember that decisions are fact sensitive. The case of *Steve Hill Ltd* should not be taken as an

130 See: Morris v Rigby (1966) 110 S.J. 834 CA (wife's sister) and Regan v Williamson [1976] 1 W.L.R. 305 (wife's aunt)

131 Spittle v Bunney [1988] 1 W.L.R 847 CA

132 [2021] EWCA Civ 1312

133 Ibid, at para 43

authority for the proposition that awards must always be made at the full commercial rate[134]. The Court will assess the value of the lost services in relation to the particular facts of the case.

Frequently the court then also considers the special quality of the care provided by the parent. This particular element of the calculations is a relatively new development and is often referred to as a "Regan v Williamson award"[135].

Claims for the loss of services of a parent or carer can often be substantial, especially where young children are involved, and it is often the case that obtaining a report from an expert in care is justified.

8.5.3 AWARDS FOR PAST LOSS OF SERVICES

An award in damages is still made for these services even if no steps have been taken to employ anyone to replace the services. It is frequently pleaded and sometimes argued that no award should be made for past loss of services (that is the loss of services up to the date of trial) where no housekeeper has in fact been hired. The argument put is that, as a matter of fact, no loss has been suffered. It is clear from reading the case law in this area from the beginning of the twentieth century that this argument is unsustainable.

The argument was rejected in the case of *Knauer v Ministry of Justice*[136] when it was heard at High Court level. In this case five years had passed since Mrs Knauer's death and Mr Knauer had not employed a cook, cleaner, gardener or decorator "still less a resident housekeeper"[137]. The

134 Ibid, at para 41.

135 Regan v Williamson [1976] 1 W.L.R. 305

136 [2014] EWHC 2553 (QB)

137 Ibid at para 25

defendant argued that in these circumstances no award should be made. The court firmly rejected this argument. Mr Justice Bean stated:

> *This submission, with respect, is misconceived, on basic principles of the law of tort. If a claimant's brand new Rolls-Royce is written off through the defendant's negligence the damages must include its replacement value even if the claimant decides that he will change to a cheaper car or in future take public transport. The same principle applies to claims for loss of services under the Fatal Accidents Acts; and to claims for future loss, though not past loss, brought by a living claimant for her own personal injuries (Daly v General Steam Navigation Ltd [1981] 1 WLR 120). Of course in a sense the value of a lost spouse cannot be measured in money terms (see Proverbs, chapter 31, verses 10 ff.) but the law has to do the best it can.*
>
> *[…]*
>
> *Indeed, Mr Poole's submission is contradicted by high authority: in Hay v Hughes [1975] QB 790 at 809B Lord Edmund-Davies said that "the fact that a widower decided to manage himself after the death of his wife would not disentitle him to sue for and recover damages for the pecuniary loss he had sustained."*

8.5.4 THE SPECIAL QUALITY OF CARE PROVIDED BY A PARENT

The love and attention provided to a child by a parent frequently goes far beyond that provided by a housekeeper or nanny or the like. It is difficult for courts to compensate for all that the child has lost in this regard solely by reference to the commercial cost of replacing the services that have been lost. This difficulty was first identified by Edmund-Davies LJ in the case of *Hay v Hughes*[138]. Since the case of *Regan v Williamson*[139] in 1976 the courts have increasingly recognised this potential further loss and made modest lump sum awards for loss of services that are above the cost of employing a housekeeper or nanny. In the case of *Regan* Watkins J stated:

> *... a wife and a mother does not work set hours and, still less, to rule. She is in constant attendance, save for those hours when she is, if that is the fact, at work. During some of those hours she may well give the children instruction on essential matters to do with their upbringing and, possibly, with such things as their homework. This sort of attention seems to be as much of a service, and probably more valuable to them, than the other kinds of service conventionally so described.*

The court went on to award a sum of money in relation to the loss of services provided by the mother which was greater than the cost of employing a replacement housekeeper. A similar approach to the quantification of the loss of services provided by a mother was adopted by the court in the case of *Mehmet v Perry*[140] where the court awarded an additional modest sum to reflect the fact that "the children have lost the attention of their mother"[141]. In *Mehmet* the court also awarded the husband a modest additional sum because he had lost the special care and attention of his wife. "Regan v Williamson" awards are discussed in more detail at chapter thirteen.

In modern litigation, in most cases which involve the loss of a mother, a "Regan v Williamson" award is claimed. This is particularly the case where the claim is brought on behalf of the child or children of the

---

138 [1975] Q.B. 790

139 [1976] 1 W.L.R. 305.

140 [1977] 2 All E.R. 529

141 Ibid at para 537f

deceased alone. There is no reason why, if the facts permit, such a claim could not be made in a case which involved the loss of a father.

The sums awarded vary but tend to be relatively modest in the context of the claim overall. In the case of *Mehmet* (which was decided in 1977) £1,500 was awarded. By 1991, in the case of *Corbett v Barking Havering and Brentwood Health Authority*[142] £3,000 was awarded with a slightly higher amount of £3,500 being awarded in the 1996 case of Johnson v British Midland Airways Ltd[143]. In the case of *H v S*[144] the trial judge initially awarded the sums of £5,000 and £7,000 where the children were 11 and 8 respectively. These sums were considered too high by the Court of Appeal and were reduced to £3,500 and £4,500 respectively. In the more recent case of *Chouza v Martins*[145] £5,000 was allowed.

There are instances where the evidence demonstrates that the quality of care provided by the deceased parent is so poor that damages are reduced on appeal. This occurred in the case of *Stanley v Saddique*[146] where the award for loss of the mother's services made by the trial judge at first instance was reduced by the Court of Appeal because the evidence showed that she provided a poor quality of care.

8.5.5 WHERE CARE IS NOW PROVIDED BY MEMBERS OF THE FAMILY

It is often the case that following the death of a family member other members of the family take over the care of children and the management of the household. Although by virtue of S4 of the Fatal Accidents Act

142 [1992] 2 QB 408

143 [1996] PIQR Q8

144 [2003] Q.B. 965 CA

145 [2021] EWHC 1669 at para 88

146 [1992] Q.B. 1

1976 any benefits arising from death must be disregarded, the case law in this area shows that claims for loss of services in these circumstances must be kept realistic.

In general there can be little doubt that the courts view the hiring of a relative to provide childcare as a reasonable step. In the past the courts have been willing to allow the cost of such a step even when it exceeded the cost of hiring professional assistance. In the case of *Morris v Rigby*[147] the widower employed the services of his deceased wife's sister to care for his children. The evidence showed that this cost more than hiring a nanny and housekeeper at market rates. The court stated that it was reasonable in the circumstances to engage the services of the deceased wife's sister despite the fact that it cost more than the market rate.

The case of *Corbett v Barking Havering and Brentwood Health Authority*[148] is a more recent case, however, and is authority for the proposition that in cases where care of the children has been taken over by surviving members of the family the cost of hiring a nanny on commercial rates is only a guide to the judge as to the figure of damages to be awarded. In this case Purchas LJ stated:

> *It must never be forgotten in this particular exercise that the multiplicand/multiplier approach based on the cost of hiring alternative commercial services is at best a very crude and approximate instrument. It borders on complete artificiality...*[149]

In the case of *Corbett* the Court of Appeal also endorsed the trial judge's approach of taking the net "in hand" cost of employing the nanny as the starting point for the cost of replacing the services.

Where a member of the family has left paid employment in order to care for the surviving children whether the court awards damages that equate

---

147 (1966) 110 S.J.834 CA

148 [1991] 2 Q.B. 408 CA

149 Ibid at page 10 para A

to the loss of earnings depends on whether the action was "reasonable". The open-ended nature of this test means that decisions on this point vary and are fact specific.

In the case of *Cresswell v Eaton*[150] it was deemed reasonable for the aunt to give up paid employment as a traffic warden. The award of damages was made in reference to the loss of salary. In the case of *Mehmet*[151] the husband had given up his job to care for his two children who suffered from a rare blood disorder. The court held it was reasonable for him to do so and awarded the loss of wages instead of the lower cost of employing a housekeeper.

By contrast, in the case of *Batt v Highgate Private Hospital*[152] the court determined that it was unreasonable for the father to leave his job to look after his daughter and damages were based on the cost of providing commercial care which was considerably below the amount claimed as loss of earnings.

8.6 HELD ON TRUST

As with other personal injury claims the sums of money awarded for voluntary services are to be held on trust for the individual providing those services. Where the court is satisfied that the sums will be used in this manner no further order in relation to this aspect of the case is made. Where there are concerns that the sums will not be used in this manner the court can take steps to enforce this trust. In the case of *ATH & Anor v MS*[153] Lord Justice Kennedy stated:

---

150 [1991] 1 W.L.R. 1113

151 Mehmet v Perry [1977] 2 All E.R. 529

152 [2005] P.I.Q.R. Q1

153 ATH & Anor v MS [2002] EWCA Civ 792

> *...such damages can only be awarded on the basis that they are used to reimburse the voluntary carer for services already rendered, and are available to pay for such services in the future. In the words used by Lord Bridge in Hunt v Severs damages are held on trust and if the terms of the trust seem unlikely to be fulfilled then the court awarding damages must take steps to avoid that outcome. Contrary to what was said by Crane J in Bordin I believe that the trust is one which the court can, and in an appropriate case should enforce.*

8.7 LOSS OF EARNINGS OF THE SURVIVING PARTNER

It is not possible to claim the loss of earnings of the surviving partner as a free-standing head of loss in a claim for dependency under the Fatal Accidents Act. This is because, as a matter of law, this loss does not flow from the relationship the surviving partner had with the deceased.

In the case of *Rupasinghe -v- West Hertfordshire Hospitals NHS Trust*[154] Jay J summarised the position:

> *"...a free-standing claim for loss of earnings falls outside the scope of section 3 of the Fatal Accidents Act 1976. This is because such a claim does not relate to the loss of a benefit which would have accrued to the Claimant had the Deceased survived. The Act is only concerned with losses which flow from what the Deceased did when alive: either by the making of a financial contribution to the household, or by providing childcare and similar services (capable, under the common law, of being accorded a financial value)."*

In reaching this conclusion, Jay J cited Diplock LJ in *Malyon v Plummer*[155]:

154 [2016] EWHC 2848 (QB)

155 [1964] 1 QB 330 at page 349

> *"It has, however, long been established...first: that the pecuniary loss to the persons for whose benefit the action is brought is the only damage recoverable, and, secondly, that the pecuniary loss recoverable is limited to the loss of a benefit in money or money's worth, which if the deceased had survived, would have accrued to a person within the defined relationship to the deceased, and would have arisen from that relationship and not otherwise."*

As set out earlier[156] the standard approach to valuing the losses in relation to providing childcare and other services is to calculate the net cost of replacing those services. However, there have been instances where the Court has seemingly followed an alternative approach of valuing those services and has done so with reference to the earnings foregone by the surviving claimant in order to provide the services.

In the case of *Mehmet v Perry*[157] the surviving partner had given up employment to take over the childcare services previously provided by the deceased. Brian Neill QC (sitting as a Deputy High Court Judge) held that it was reasonable for the damages for the loss of the deceased's services to be assessed by reference to the plaintiff's loss of wages. In the case of *Rupasinghe* two other instances of unreported cases where the Court was prepared to take a similar approach are also discussed: *Steer v Basu*[158] and *Watkins v Lovegrove*[159]. It seems clear that in all these cases the Court determined that the amount being claimed as a loss of earnings claim stood as a reasonable approximation of the value of the deceased's services and made an award on that basis[160]. As Jay J states *"This is not a claim for loss of earnings in the strict sense; it is a claim for loss of services but*

156 See 8.5.2

157 [1977] 2 All ER 529

158 [an unreported decision of Caulfield J decided in 1968]

159 [unreported, 5th May 1982]

160 See discussion in *Rupasinghe* Op cit at paragraphs 24-55

using the surviving partner's earnings as a proxy or surrogate measure for the value of the services foregone."[161]

By contrast, in the case of *Rupasinghe* the claimant was advancing a claim for loss of earnings which was in addition to the cost of replacing the services of the deceased. The claim for lost services had already been compromised and Dr Rupasinghe was advancing an additional claim because she had lost her career because of her husband's death.

Jay J concluded:

> *"The disputed items do not constitute an attempt by the Claimant, applying some form of proxy measure, to value the loss of the Deceased's services, but rather a broader endeavour predicated on reasoning that the Claimant has lost her career because of her husband's untimely death. That is, of course, correct as a matter of fact, but it does not avail her as a matter of law. Seen in these terms, the claim is indeed one for loss of earnings, not one attributable to any need to replace a service that the Deceased had formerly been providing."*[162]

8.8 SUMMARY

In summary:

a) A claim for dependency is a claim for the loss of the pecuniary benefit arising from the relationship that the dependant had with the deceased;

b) This pecuniary benefit can be in the form of money or services or both;

161 Ibid at paragraph 50

162 Ibid at paragraph 52.

c) Claims for bereavement, funeral expenses, the pain suffering and loss of amenity of the deceased and other losses of the deceased are not part of a dependency claim but can form the subject of other claims under the Fatal Accidents Act 1976 and the Law Reform (Miscellaneous Provisions) Act 1934;

d) The general approach to calculating dependency is by a multiplicand and multiplier process;

e) In the relatively rare instances where mathematical calculations return a result which is obviously at odds with the facts of the case, the court is not bound to blindly follow the mathematical approach;

f) The starting point when calculating the amount of money earned by the deceased is usually the annual salary the deceased was earning at the time of death;

g) In addition to the salary itself, other benefits from the employment should be taken into account;

h) The court will take into account the fact that the deceased's wage would have been likely to rise or fall in the future;

i) If the deceased received state benefits these can be included in the loss of earning capacity calculation;

j) In circumstances where the deceased was a businessman or similar, arguments are often advanced by the defendant that because the business survives the deceased and continues to generate revenue the dependants have not suffered any financial loss. This argument rarely succeeds;

k) A claim can also be advanced for the loss of holidays, gifts and luxuries provided by the deceased;

l) In addition to the loss of income, a loss of dependency claim includes the cost of replacing the services the deceased provided to the dependants;

m) Claims for loss of services often focus on the loss of childcare services but claims can be made for loss of services that the deceased provided free of charge such as (but not limited to) DIY services and gardening;

n) The starting point for calculating the cost of replacing the services is the net cost of replacing the services by hiring a professional;

o) The court can also make a Regan v Williamson award to account for the special quality of the care provided by the parent that has been lost;

p) The sums of money awarded for voluntary services are to be held on trust for the individual providing those services.

CHAPTER NINE

THE REDUCTION FOR PERSONAL EXPENDITURE

9.1 INTRODUCTION

> *Then there is an estimate of how much was required or expended for his own personal and living expenses.*[163]

Once the likely annual value of the deceased's salary or earnings has been ascertained, a calculation is performed to deduct the sum that the deceased spent solely on themselves. This chapter considers the conventional approach to this deduction, cases where the conventional approach has been departed from and the different approaches the court adopts for different family circumstances.

9.2 THE CONVENTIONAL APPROACH

Over time a conventional approach has developed for this calculation, as confirmed by the case of *Harris v Empress Motors*[164]. This conventional approach is not always the correct approach, but it remains useful in a great number of cases. It is used in situations where one partner in a relationship is working and the other is not.

The *Harris v Empress Motors* approach to removing the amount of the salary or earnings that the deceased spent on themselves is as follows:

---

163 Davies v Powell Duffryn Associated Collieries Ltd [1942] AC 601 at 617

164 [1983] 3 All E.R. 561

a) 33.3% is deducted from the amount if the deceased had no children and left only a dependent partner or spouse;

b) 25% is deducted from the amount if the deceased has left a dependent partner and spouse and dependent children[165].

So, where the deceased was earning £10,000 net per year and left a dependent wife, the sum of £10,000 is reduced by 33.3% to £6,666.67. Where the deceased was earning £10,000 net a year and left a dependent wife and children, the sum is reduced by 25% to £7,500.

9.3 THE EARNINGS OF THE SPOUSE OR PARTNER

A slightly different calculation is performed where, before the death, the surviving partner was working and continues to do so following the death. In these circumstances:

a) The net joint income of the couple is calculated;

b) 66% of the net joint income is calculated;

c) The net earnings of the surviving spouse or partner are then deducted to give a final annual figure for dependency.

So, where the deceased was earning £10,000 net and his wife was earning £10,000 net a year the joint income is £20,000. Two thirds of £20,000 is £13,333. The surviving wife's wage of £10,000 is then deducted leaving a sum of £3,333 as the annual figure for dependency.

165 The basis for this smaller deduction is that the money the deceased earned was presumed to be split four ways instead of three; ¼ for the deceased, ¼ for the child or children, ¼ for the wife and ¼ for joint use.

9.4 DEPARTURES FROM THE CONVENTIONAL APPROACH

The approach in *Harris* is the conventional approach and should be used unless there is clear evidence that to do so would result in an unfair award. In *Harris* Lord Justice O'Connor stated:

> *The percentages have become conventional in the sense that they are used unless there is striking evidence to make the conventional figure inappropriate because there is no departure from the principle that each case must be decided upon its facts.*[166]

Instances which merit a departure from the *Harris* approach will be relatively rare. An example is the case of *Martin & Ors v Owen*[167] when the claimant was a young childless widow whose husband had died within a year of their marriage. The claimant had committed adultery with two different men in the previous four or five years. The Court of Appeal departed from the conventional approach as they stated it was "plain" that it was unlikely the widow's dependency would remain at two thirds of the deceased's earnings for the whole of his working life. In the case Stuart Smith LJ stated:

> *Such a rule of thumb [the conventional approach] will not be appropriate where the husband is a high earner who may well spend a higher proportion on himself. Nor is it appropriate in the case of a young childless widow.*[168]

In the case of *Coward v Comex Houlder Diving Ltd*[169] the Court of Appeal departed from the conventional approach and allowed an increased percentage for dependency. This was on the basis that the deceased

---

166 Ibid at page 7F

167 [1992] P.I.Q.R. Q151 CA

168 Ibid at para 160

169 (Unreported) Lawtel; Independent, July 25, 1988

worked as a diver in the North Sea for extended periods of time and as such spent less of his earnings solely on himself.

More recently, in the case of Chouza v Martins[170] the Court departed from the conventional approach. In that case the Court departed from the conventional percentages (75% and 66%) and adjusted them to 85% pre-retirement and 70% post retirement.

Mr Justice Martin Spencer cited the case *Owen v Martin*[171] (1992) WL 895670:

> *"O'Connor LJ did not intend to lay down any rule that in the absence of striking evidence to the contrary two thirds of net income must be regarded as the value of the dependency I have no doubt. If he did he would clearly have been wrong. It is clear that the value of the dependency cannot be taken at such an arbitrary figure and must always depend on facts."*[172]

The Defendant argued that absent clear documentary evidence on the level of expenditure the Court could not move past the "*conventional percentages of 75% (with dependant children) and 66% (husband and wife alone)*"[173].

Mr Justice Martin Spencer disagreed and stated:

> *"a distinction needs to be drawn between 2 aspects: first, as referred to by O'Connor LJ in Harris, there is the methodology, namely whether the court embarks upon a painstaking and tedious examination of the household expenses or whether it adopts a more broad-brush percentage approach; second, if the percentage approach is to be adopted, what the appropriate percentage should be in any*

170 [2021] EWHC 1669 (QB)

171 [1992] WL 895670

172 *Chouza*, Op Cit at para 48

173 Ibid, at para 49

> *particular case...O'Connor LJ only intended to suggest that the absence of the painstaking or tedious approach should lead to a broader, percentage approach, but not necessarily to what those percentages should be. If the court decides on the percentage approach, it may be more ready to depart from the conventional percentages on the basis of more general evidence about the lifestyles of the family and adjust the percentages accordingly. In other words, it is not necessary, in order to depart from the conventional percentages, to descend into the nitty-gritty of the family finances and work out precisely how much was spent on the various individual items of expenditure."*[174]

We should be cautious about reading *Chouza* as stating that the Court will readily agree to moving away from the conventional percentage deductions. The facts in *Chouza* were unusual and the Claimant had marshalled detailed and specific evidence on the point[175].

It remains the case that the starting point is the conventional deductions. In the 2024 case of *Price v Marstons Plc*[176], having observed that the task of the Court is to use whatever material is available to best determine the extent of the loss, Mr Justice Griffiths observed:

> *"But this does not mean that the court should start from scratch and ignore the tools that earlier cases have provided to accomplish a task which is necessarily based on counter factual and hypothetical speculation about what would have happened if the fatal accident in question had not occurred. The point of actuarial and statistical tools such as those based on the Ogden tables and of the two thirds / one third rule of thumb is that they counterbalance the uncertainties that would exist in a single case, were it to be looked at in isolation, by averaging over countless examples from other similar cases in order to produce a result which is reliable notwithstanding the uncertainties*

---

174 Ibid at para 49

175 Ibid at para 46

176 [2024] EWHC 1352 (KB)

of the case. It is precisely because the task is difficult and speculative that these tools have been developed, and are of such value. They are not, lightly, to be discarded, especially if an unconventional approach leads to a result which does not seem correct or fair. This is a point made in Cape Distribution v O'Loughlin [2001] EWCA Civ 178, by Judge LJ (with whom Schiemann LJ agreed) at para 26: "I merely sound the cautionary note that where the court is invited to adopt an unusual or unconventional approach in a case of this kind, an additional burden is imposed on the judge to ensure that the more conventional approach would not provide the fairest way to do justice between the parties, and, even if he is satisfied that it would not, he should stand back from the figure to which the unconventional approach had led him and examine whether it fairly reflected the practical realities of the case."[177]

9.4.2 A WORKING SPOUSE OR PARTNER WHO GIVES UP WORK AFTER THE DEATH

Where the spouse or partner was in work before the deceased's death but following the death gives up work, the court can still take into account the earnings before death in calculating the dependency.

In the case of *Taylor v Prosol Façade Access Ltd*[178] the wife had given up her job following her husband's death partly as a result of the psychological upset caused by the death and also to concentrate on looking after her children. HHJ David Wilcox stated:

In my judgment, the wife's earning capacity, logically must be taken into account in assessing her dependency if the evidence, at the time of death, impels the reasonable inference that both would have earned and contributed had the deceased lived [...]The relevant

177 Ibid at para 137

178 [2003] EWHC 310 TTC

> *consideration under the Fatal Accidents Act is: 'what would have happened in relation to her employment had the deceased remained alive?'; not 'what the widow is now constrained to do in consequence of his death'.*[179]

If the surviving partner or spouse has given up work to care for the children, and this is deemed a reasonable step by the court, a claim can be advanced for the loss of salary. For a full discussion of this area see chapter eight[180].

9.4.3 POTENTIAL EARNINGS OF THE SURVIVING PARTNER

The dependency claim is fixed at the time of death[181]. The key question is what was the other partner's intention "but for" the death. If when the deceased was alive the other partner did not work and had no intention of working, then this is the basis on which the court calculates the loss of dependency claim. The court ignores the future earning potential of the surviving partner. In these circumstances an argument that the court should consider the future potential earning power of a surviving partner is misconceived[182]. This is the case even where, following the death but before trial, the surviving partner has actually started to work.

In the case of *Howitt v Heads*[183] the court held that the widow's potential for future employment must be excluded from the calculation of the loss

179 Ibid at paras 19 and 21

180 At Chapter 8.5.5

181 Welsh Ambulance Services NHS Trust v Williams [2008] EWCA Civ 81

182 The comment in Cookson v Knowles [1977] Q.B. 913 CA at 922E by Lord Denning where he states that the court is "not so sure" about ignoring the fact that the widow could go out to work is obiter. The case of Welsh Ambulance Services is clear recent authority.

183 [1973] Q.B. 64

of dependency damages. In the cases of *Davies v Whiteways Cyder Co*[184] and *Dodds v Dodds*[185] the dependant had actually returned to work and earned money in between the death and the trial but this was excluded from the calculation of the loss of dependency damages.

If the evidence shows that when the deceased was alive the other partner always had plans to return to work in the future (for example after the children had left home or after a planned career break) then this should be reflected in the dependency calculation.

9.5 SUMMARY

In summary:

a) Once the likely annual level of the deceased's salary or earnings has been ascertained, a calculation is performed to deduct the sum that the deceased spent solely on themselves;

b) The case of *Harris v Empress Motors* sets out the conventional approach to removing the amount of the salary or earnings that the deceased spent on themselves;

c) A slightly different calculation is performed where, before the death, the surviving partner was working and continues to do so following the death;

d) The approach in *Harris* is the conventional approach and should be used unless there is clear evidence that to do so would result in an unfair award;

e) In particular factual circumstances the Court can depart from the conventional approach and can still do so on a "broad brush" basis

184 [1975] Q.B. 262

185 [1978] Q.B. 543

without the need for descending to the "nitty gritty" detail of the family finances;

f) Where the spouse or partner was in work before the deceased's death but following the death gives up work, the court can still take into account the earnings before death in calculating the dependency;

g) The dependency claim is fixed at the time of death[186]. The key question is what was the other partner's intention "but for" the death.

186 Welsh Ambulance Services NHS Trust v Williams [2008] EWCA Civ 81

CHAPTER TEN

THE MULTIPLIER

10.1 INTRODUCTION

The multiplier is a figure which is based on the amount of time in years that the dependency is likely to continue for. This figure is then reduced to account for the fact that the claimant will be receiving the damages as one lump sum. The multiplier can also be reduced to account for other contingencies.

The starting point for the multiplier is the number of years the dependency would have continued for if the deceased had not died. Often different multipliers are used for different periods of dependency; one multiplier for the period the children will be dependent and another for the period of time when the widow will be dependent[187]. This chapter discusses the starting point for the calculation of the multiplier and the range of considerations which may affect the calculation.

10.2 THE STARTING POINT FOR THE MULTIPLIER

There has been much criticism of the decision in the case of *Cookson v Knowles*[188]. In that case the House of Lords affirmed the decision of the Court of Appeal in the same case that the multiplier in Fatal Accidents Act cases was set from the date of death. This position has now been

---

187 For a reported example of this see the cases of Young v Percival [1975] 1 W.L.R. 17 CA and Robertson v Lestrange [1985] 1 All E.R. 950

188 [1979] A.C 556 affirming [1977] Q.B 913 CA. See, as one example, The Law Commission (Law Com No 263) Claims for Wrongful Death November 1999 Part IV

overturned by the decision of the Supreme Court in the case of *Knauer (a widower and administrator of the estate of Sally Ann Knauer) v Ministry of Justice*[189]: the multiplier is now set from the date of trial.

The difficulty with the previous practice of setting the multiplier from the date of death was that there was the danger of undercompensating the claimant dependant. One of the main functions for using a multiplier is to take into account the fact that the claimant is receiving the damages as a lump sum rather than in increments over the years. This is called a "discount for early receipt". A discount for early receipt only needs to be applied to future losses, i.e. losses from the date of the trial. Losses that have already been incurred before the matter arrives at trial are past losses and there has been no "early receipt" when damages are awarded for them.

By using a multiplier assessed at the date of trial, which was then adjusted for the number of years between the death and the trial, the court was building a discount for early receipt into the past damages. This was unfair because there had been no early receipt of these damages. As the Supreme Court put it in the case of *Knauer*:

> *Calculating damages for loss of dependency upon the deceased from the date of death, rather than from the date of trial, means that the claimant is suffering a discount for early receipt of the money when in fact that money will not be received until after trial.[...] as the figures in this case show, the effect of the discount for the non-existent early receipt of the money is far from negligible. It results in under-compensation in most cases.*[190]

The case of *Knauer* makes it very clear that the new Ogden tables in relation to fatal accidents are now the correct starting point for the

189 [2016] UKSC 9

190 Ibid at para 7

calculation of multipliers in fatal accident cases. These multipliers are used for both past and future losses.

The Ogden tables are a set of statistical tables for use in court cases. The first edition was published in 1984 and they are now into their 7th edition. At the time of publication of the 7th edition the case of *Cookson* remained good law but the 7th edition of the Ogden tables include at section D a detailed explanation of the "actuarially recommended approach" to calculating the multiplier in fatal accident cases along with the relevant tables to apply the recommended discounts to multipliers. A full discussion of the manner in which Ogden tables are compiled and calculated and how they operate is beyond the scope of this work. A thorough understanding of the principles behind the Ogden tables is necessary for even the most straightforward of fatal accident cases. As is noted in the commentary to the Ogden tables themselves, in very large claims or claims where the accuracy of the multiplier is of crucial importance the advice of an actuary should be sought. The relevant Ogden tables and explanatory notes can be found in free PDF format at https://www.gov.uk/government/publications/ogden-tables-actuarial-compensation-tables-for-injury-and-death.

10.3 PAST LOSSES

Past losses are losses that have been incurred from the date of death up until the date of trial. Some of these losses will be an annual loss of dependency. The process of calculating the multiplier for these past losses is as follows:

a) The number of years between the date of death and trial is calculated;

b) This number is then discounted by the relevant factor in tables set out in chapter A7 of Facts and Figures 25/26[191].

The discount is accounting for the risk that the deceased would have died in any event before the trial. Because the chance of this is usually, statistically, very small the discount is often very small and sometimes non-existent. No discount is applied when the deceased was 40 or under at the time of death. Greater discounts occur when the deceased was already in old age because the chance of them dying in any event is obviously greater.

10.4 FUTURE LOSSES

Future losses are, obviously, losses which will occur after the trial date. The process of calculating the multiplier for future losses is as follows:

a) Multipliers are based on either how long the deceased would have been able to provide the dependency or how long the dependant would have received the dependency; whichever is the shorter period;

b) This period is then treated as a term certain for which the multiplier is to be determined. This figure is then looked up in Table 36 of the Ogden tables[192].

c) Any further contingencies other than mortality are then applied in accordance with section B of the Ogden tables.

191 A7: Table of adjustments to multiplier for Fatal Accidents Act dependency – Factor by which pre-trial damages should be multiplied to allow for the likelihood that the deceased would not in any case have survived to provide the dependency for the full period to the date of trial.

192 Multipliers for pecuniary loss for term certain in 2025/26 edition of Facts and Figures

d) If necessary this multiplier can then discounted further to account for the risk that the deceased may have died anyway before the date of trial. This is done by applying the relevant factor in chapter A7 of Facts and Figures.

How the Court arrives at the answers to the two questions in part a) above is discussed in more detail below.

10.5 FOR HOW LONG WOULD THE DECEASED HAVE BEEN ABLE TO PROVIDE THE DEPENDENCY?

The calculation of the multiplier for future losses will usually require the court to determine how long the deceased would have lived for, in the absence of the event that killed him, and for how long the deceased would have worked. The Ogden tables deal with life expectancy and following *Knauer* there can be little doubt that their application is as valid in fatal accident cases as in personal injury cases.

The Ogden tables deal with the average life expectancy. There is scope for the defendant to argue that there should be a departure from the average life expectancy because of particular features of the deceased's lifestyle. He who asserts must prove and as such it is for the defendant to prove that a specific feature of the deceased's lifestyle merits a departure from the average. This principle should be uncontroversial, as long ago as 1873 it was clarified in the case of *Rowley v London and N.W Ry*[193] where the court held that, in the absence of the defendant establishing that special circumstances existed, the jury were properly directed to consider the life as an average life. The most common factors which it is argued should merit a departure from the average life are bad health and hazardous employment.

193 (1873) L.R. 8 Ex 221

10.6 FOR HOW LONG WOULD THE DEPENDANT HAVE RECEIVED THE DEPENDENCY?

This question is most frequently a feature in cases where a parent has died, and the child is claiming dependency. It can also arise in other situations such as where the deceased was the carer to an adult dependant. How long a child will be dependent is a fact-specific question that depends on the evidence of a particular case.

The courts have made a variety of different decisions on how long a child will be dependent on the deceased. In the case of *K v J.M.P Co*[194] the Court of Appeal accepted the judge at first instance that the child's dependency should be limited to 16. In the case of *Cresswell v Eaton*[195] the dependency was limited to 18 for one child and 22 for the younger child who was deemed to be brighter and more likely to be educated to a tertiary level. In *Corbett v Barking Havering and Brentwood Health Authority*[196] the trial judge set the dependency past the age of 18 on the basis that the chances of the child proceeding to university were evenly balanced. On appeal the Court of Appeal adjusted this slightly by increasing the multiplier by one. In the case of *H v S*[197] the judge at first instance set the dependency until the age of 24 on the basis that both boys would be at university until that time. This was reduced by the Court of Appeal to 21 to account for the contingency that one or other of the boys might not proceed to university.

Although there are no reported cases that demonstrate this (the majority of Fatal Accidents cases being settled before trial) this author has experience of dependency claims succeeding well past the mid-twenties and even into the thirties and beyond when the facts of the case permit. As the trend for children to attend tertiary education and then return

194 [1975] 1 All ER 1030, CA

195 [1991] 1 W.L.R. 1113

196 [1991] 2 Q.B. 408 CA

197 [2003] Q.B. 965 CA

home for a period increases, such claims are likely to become more prevalent.

A further consideration for the court when assessing how long a child would have remained dependent on their parents is the likelihood of the child marrying. The argument is that when the child has married, they will cease to be dependent on the parent(s). This has been taken into account by the court in cases involving a dependent son in the cases of *Dolbey v Goodwin*[198] and *Wathen v Vernon*[199]. The same consideration is clearly relevant for dependent daughters of the deceased.

As discussed above at chapter seven the prospect of a widow or widower remarrying is now completely excluded from calculations[200].

10.6.1 PROSPECT OF DIVORCE

It seems clear that, when assessing the appropriate multiplier to apply, the court can take into account, the fact that a relationship may have been fragile and might have ended in divorce.

The case of *Martin & Ors v Owen*[201] has already been discussed at chapter nine[202]. We can recall that the facts of that case were that the claimant was a young childless widow whose husband had died within a year of their marriage and that the claimant had committed adultery with two different men in the past four or five years. The Court of Appeal reversed the decision of the judge at first instance who held that the prospects of divorce must be left to one side when considering the multiplier. The

198 [1955] 1 W.L.R. 553 CA

199 [1970] R.T.R 471 CA

200 See chapter 7.2.3

201 [1992] P.I.Q.R. Q151 CA

202 See chapter 9.3

Court of Appeal held that the statutory provision in the Fatal Accidents Act 1976 which stated the prospects of remarriage must be disregarded did not apply in the context of considering the fragility of the marriage at the time of death. The Court of Appeal reduced the multiplier of 15 (which was suitable for a widow "married for an appreciable time whose marriage could be said to have stood the test of time and whose pecuniary advantage to her deceased husband was settled and assured") with a multiplier of 10.

A further example of the court reducing the multiplier to take account of the prospects of divorce can be found in the case of *D and D v Donald*[203]. In that case it was the deceased husband's actions which the court found gave rise to the likelihood of divorce as opposed to the widow's actions.

In the case of CC v TD[204] HHJ Freedman (sitting as a Judge of the High Court) held that where a husband and wife were in the middle of divorce proceedings when he was killed in a road accident, the wife's claim for loss of financial dependency was limited to what she would have received in post-divorce maintenance payments. He rejected the Claimant's contention that they would have reconciled and found that the chances of this were "no more than a speculative possibility"[205].

10.6.2 PROSPECT OF RECONCILIATION

As we have seen above, it is sometimes argued that although at the time of death the relationship had broken down, but for the death a reconciliation would have occurred, and damages should be assessed on this basis.

203 [2001] P.I.Q.R. Q5 p.44

204 [2018] EWHC 1240 (QB)

205 Ibid, paragraph 52

In the case of *Davies v Taylor*[206] the House of Lords dealt with the issue of reconciliation. In that case the plaintiff's husband was killed in a road accident caused by the defendant's negligence. She had deserted him five weeks before his death and after she had left, he learned about her adultery with a fellow employee. He tried to effect reconciliation with her, but she refused. Shortly before his death, he had instructed his solicitor to institute divorce proceedings.

The case of *Davies* sets out a two-stage test that a claimant must satisfy. Firstly, the claimant must establish that the chance of reconciliation was substantial. It is important to note that the claimant does not need to establish that reconciliation would have occurred on the balance of probabilities. The chance of reconciliation can be less than 50%. See chapter 6.5 for further discussion on the concept of substantial chance as expressed in *Davies.*

If the claimant establishes a substantial chance of reconciliation, then the Court must evaluate what the prospect of reconciliation was in percentage terms. The dependency claim is then awarded at this percentage. So, for example, where the Claimant has established that there is a substantial chance of reconciliation and the Court has evaluated the prospect of this occurring at 80%, the Claimant would receive 80% of the dependency claim.

In the case of *Hayes -v- South East Coast Ambulance Service NHS Foundation Trust*[207] the claimant and the deceased had divorced but had recently *"resumed an intimate relationship… [and] begun to discuss the future, including remarriage"*[208]. HHJ Coe (sitting as a High Court Judge) found the prospect of reconciliation was 90% but reduced damages by a further 10% because he accepted *"that there would have to be some reduction to reflect the fact that there would be a risk that even having*

206 [1974] AC 207

207 [2015] EWHC 18 (QB)

208 Ibid, paragraph 147

reconciled the relationship would have failed again"[209]. In relation to Mrs Hayes' dependency claim[210] damages were awarded at 80% of the full amount.

10.7 CIVIL PARTNERSHIPS

We have already discussed above at chapter six the fact that the Fatal Accidents Act 1976 contains a specific provision regarding civil partnerships and cohabitees[211]. The Act requires the court to take into account the fact that the deceased and the dependant were not married when considering the appropriate multiplier to be applied. For the sake of completeness it is worth setting out this principle again. Section 3(4) of the Fatal Accidents Act 1976 states:

> *In an action under this Act where there fall to be assessed damages payable to a person who is a dependant by virtue of section 1(3)(b) above in respect of the death of the person with whom the dependant was living as husband or wife or civil partner there shall be taken into account (together with any other matter that appears to the court to be relevant to the action) the fact that the dependant had no enforceable right to financial support by the deceased as a result of their living together.*

In the case of *Drew v Abassi*[212] the Court of Appeal upheld a decision where the trial judge reduced the multiplier from 15 to 13 to take account of the fact that the dependant in question was not married but was a common law spouse.

---

209 Ibid, paragraph 148

210 The children's dependency claims were unaffected by the prospect of reconciliation.

211 See chapter 6.3.6

212 (Unreported, CA, 24 May 1995)

10.8 SUMMARY

In summary:

a) The multiplier is a figure which is based on the amount of time in years that the dependency is likely to continue for;

b) The starting point for the multiplier is the number of years the dependency would have continued for if the deceased had not died;

c) The calculation of the multiplier for future losses will often require the court to determine how long the deceased would have lived for, in the absence of the event that killed him, and for how long the deceased would have worked;

d) How long a child will be dependent is a fact-specific question that depends on the evidence of a particular case;

e) Following the case of *Knauer*[213] the multiplier is now set from the date of trial;

f) This figure is then reduced to account for the fact that the claimant will be receiving the damages as one lump sum;

g) The multiplier can also be reduced to account for other contingencies including the risk that the deceased may have died anyway before the date of trial;

h) When assessing the appropriate multiplier to apply, the court can take into account, the fact that a relationship may have been fragile and might have ended in divorce;

i) Section 3(4) of the Fatal Accidents Act 1976 requires the court to take into account the fact that the deceased and the dependant were

---

213 [2016] UKSC 9

not married when considering the appropriate multiplier to be applied.

CHAPTER ELEVEN

LOSS OF A CHILD: DEPENDENCY CLAIMS BY PARENTS

11.1 INTRODUCTION

In addition to the statutory bereavement award and funeral expenses (see chapter fourteen and fifteen), where the facts permit, a parent may also make a claim for loss of dependency where the deceased was their own child.

11.2 THE HISTORICAL POSITION

Historically there is considerable precedent for this type of claim where the child has been an adult. Indeed some of the earliest examples of successful claims under the Fatal Accident Act legislation involved claims made by a parent for a loss of dependency following the death of their adult child who was contributing to the family finances[214]. There are also a number of reported cases where the court found on the facts that an adult child would make regular financial contributions to their parents in the future as their parents aged[215].

---

214 See: Franklin v S.E Railway and Dalton v S.E Railway op cit.

215 See: Rowley v L. & N.W. Ry (1873) L.R. 8 Ex 221; Zinovieff v British Transport Commission [1955] 1 All E.R. 511 and Burgess v Florence Nightingale Hospital op cit.

The cases of *Taff Vale Ry v Jenkins*[216] and *Buckland v Guildford Gas Light and Coke Co*[217] show that historically the courts have been receptive to the argument that where the deceased was an adolescent child who had not yet contributed to the household but was about to, an award for loss of financial dependency should be made. Conversely where the child was an infant the court refused to make an award for loss of financial dependency because the likelihood of a pecuniary benefit arising was speculative[218].

The reported cases in this area tend to be old and probably reflect the social norms of the time. Over time, as the emphasis for the care of ageing parents has shifted from their children towards the state and pension provision, the number of reported cases where this head of loss has been awarded seems to decrease.

11.3 MORE RECENT CASES

Where particular factual circumstances permit, a claim by a parent where the deceased was their own child can still be successful. A recent example of this is the case of *Amin v Imran Khan & Partners*[219]. This case was a professional negligence case against the solicitors firm. The court found that if the matter had been dealt with properly by the defendant:

> *It was indeed possible that the dependency claim could have been regarded as very small, but it was also possible that a properly mounted claim, supported by an employment consultant's figures and*

216 [1913] A.C.

217 [1949] 1 K.B. 410

218 Barnett v Cohen [1921] 2 K.B. 461

219 [2011] EWHC 2958 (QB)

> *family evidence, could have given rise to a substantial and properly pleaded dependency*[220]

The court went on to find that, given the cultural background of the family, there was a small chance of the child making payments to his parents before they retired and that these payments would have continued on a monthly basis after retirement.

11.4 A "LUMP SUM" APPROACH

In the case of *Davies v Taylor*[221] the deceased was an adult child with special needs. The dependency claim was advanced by his parents who argued that when the father retired the deceased would have moved back into the family home and contributed to the family finances. The trial judge rejected this part of the claim on the basis that it could not be established on the balance of probabilities that such a dependency was likely to occur. The Court of Appeal reversed this decision but declined to make an award based on a multiplier and multiplicand approach and instead made an award in the sum of £5,000.

The more recent case of *Bhawsar v Ahmed*[222] is another example of the court rejecting the multiplier and multiplicand approach when making an award for loss of financial dependency following the death of an adult child. In this case the court adopted a lump sum method because of the "imponderables" in the case and awarded a total of £80,000 for loss of dependency.

220 Ibid at para 67

221 [1974] AC 207

222 [2004] All ER (D) 74

11.5 SUMMARY

In summary:

a) A claim can be advanced for loss of financial and service dependency where the deceased is an adult child;

b) Whether such a claim will succeed will depend on the facts of the case;

c) The claimant dependant must establish that the chance of such a dependency relationship arising or persisting was more than a speculative possibility;

d) Where the facts of the case contain many "imponderables" then the court is unlikely to adopt a multiplier and multiplicand approach but instead award a lump sum.

CHAPTER TWELVE

APPORTIONMENT

12.1 INTRODUCTION

As shown in chapter three above only one action may be brought on behalf of all the dependants of the deceased[223]. Because only one sum is awarded, after the court has determined the correct total amount of damages, this amount is then apportioned between the different dependants. In this chapter the principles of apportionment are discussed.

12.2 THE TOTAL AMOUNT

By far the most common approach of the court is to assess the loss to all of the dependants as a whole and then apportion this total amount between the various dependants. This approach is implied by the wording of section 3(1) of the Fatal Accidents Act 1976 which states:

> *In the action such damages, other than damages for bereavement, may be awarded as are proportioned to the injury resulting from the death to the dependants respectively.*

The court may also consider the loss of each dependant independently and then add up each dependant's loss to arrive at a total[224]. Although some commentators (very sensibly) point out the advantages of such an approach, it is still a relatively rare approach.

---

223 See chapter 3.3.2

224 Yelland v Powell Duffryn Collieries [1941] 1 K.B. 519 CA

12.3 A PRAGMATIC APPROACH TO APPORTIONMENT

It is difficult to trace any hard and fast legal principles that explain the manner in which the court approaches apportionment. There is no statutory guidance on the point. In general in cases which involve a widow (or widower) and surviving children, the normal practice of the court is to allocate the majority of the damages to the widow of the deceased. A number of reasons for this approach can be suggested:

a) There is the fact that the widow's dependency will continue for her entire life; whereas the children's dependency will cease or diminish as they grow older and become more independent;

b) There is the fact that the court may assume that the widow will use part of the damages allocated for her use for the children[225];

c) Finally, there is the practical reason that the widow (as an adult) can have immediate access to the damages whereas the children (as minors) would have the funds invested for them in the court's special account and then have to make an application for a payment out of those funds.

Within this broad approach, reported cases show a range of different approaches to apportionment, with the percentages apportioned to each individual dependant being determined by the facts of the case[226]. In general younger children are awarded a greater percentage of the damages to account for the fact that their dependency is going to persist for a longer period of time.

Where the only dependants are adults there is no need for the court to apportion damages if they agree, or plan to agree, on how to apportion the damages between themselves[227]. In the unfortunate circumstances

225 Thompson v Price [1973] Q.B. 838

226 See Kemp & Kemp Vol 2

227 Welsh Ambulance Services NHS Trust v Williams op cit

that adult dependants disagree on how the amount should be apportioned each dependant will require separate representation. It is possible for an individual dependant to appeal the amount of damages that has been awarded to them and for the appeal court to increase the amount awarded to that particular dependant without altering the amount awarded to the other dependants[228].

The procedure in relation to apportionment is set out at rule 41.3A of the CPR. Where one of the dependants is a child or a patient approval of the amount by the court is required.

Overall it is clear that when approaching the apportionment of damages the court is striving for a pragmatic approach. Latham J stated in the case of *R v Criminal Injuries Compensation Board ex parte Barrett*[229]:

> *The approach to the apportionment of the overall figure has essentially been pragmatic; the courts have sought to provide as much money in free cash terms for the parent who is caring for the child as is sensible in the circumstances, so that there can be ready access for that parent to the fund representing the lost dependency. The bulk has therefore been apportioned to the parent. [...] And it is right to say that this has never been reduced to any coherent or sensible principle.*[230]

12.4 SUMMARY

In summary:

228 Mead v Clarke Chapman [1956] 1 W.L.R. 76 CA

229 [1994] 1 F.L.R. 587

230 Ibid at para 48

a) In cases where there are dependent children and a surviving widow(er) the courts' general approach is to allocate the majority of damages to the widow;

b) Younger children generally are allocated a larger amount of the damages because their dependency will persist for longer;

c) If there are only adult dependants and they agree, or plan to agree, on how to apportion the damages then the court does not have to apportion the damages;

d) An individual dependant can appeal the amount of damages that has been awarded to him or her without the other dependants' damages being affected;

e) The procedure in relation to apportionment is set out at rule 41.3A of the CPR;

f) Where one of the dependants is a child or a patient approval of the amount by the court is required.

CHAPTER THIRTEEN

LOSS OF CONSORTIUM

13.1 INTRODUCTION

In this chapter awards of damages awarded under the principle derived from the case of *Regan v Williamson*[231] are discussed. The historical background to this type of award is summarised; the nature of this type of award is analysed; the levels of awards that have been made in the past are set out; the grounds for making such an award are considered and instances where the court has declined to make such an award are examined. A further discussion of this type of award in relation to the special quality of care provided by a parent can be found at chapter 8.5.4.

13.2 HISTORICAL BACKGROUND

The first mention of this type of award is in the case of *Berry v Humm & Co*[232]. That case concerned the 1846 Fatal Accidents Act[233]. The case of *Hay v Hughes*[234] considered this type of award more recently. In that case Edmund-Davies LJ stated:

> *"whilst it is undoubtedly the case that damages under the fatal accidents act can only be awarded in respect of pecuniary loss and not as a solatium for injured feelings...it may sometime have to be considered whether Mr McGregor is not right in saying..."it may be*

231 [1976] 1 WLR 305

232 [1915] K.B. 627

233 Ibid, paras 629-631

234 [1975] Q.B. 790

> *argued that the benefit of a mother's personal attention to a child's upbringing, morals, education and psychology, which the services of a housekeeper, nurse, or governess could never provide, has in the long run a financial value for the child, difficult as it is to assess"*[235].

Watkins J cited the case of *Hay* in the case of *Regan* the following year and stated:

> *"While I think that the law inhibits me from, much as I should like to, going all the way along the path to which Edmund-Davies pointed, I am...of the view that the word "services" has been too narrowly construed. It should, at least, include an acknowledgement that a wife and mother does not work to set hours and, still less, to rule. She is in constant attendance...she may well give the children instruction on essential matters to do with their upbringing and, possibly, with such things as their homework. This sort of attention seems to be as much of a service, and probably more valuable to them, than the other kinds of service conventionally so regarded"*[236]

The case of Regan was a first instance decision and so is not binding. There have been differing approaches taken by the Courts to this type of award, as we shall see below.

13.3 THE NATURE OF THE AWARD

This type of award is a common law award which has developed relatively recently in the context of claims arising out of fatal accidents. It is referred to variously as an award for "loss of consortium"; an award for an award for "the loss of the deceased's love and affection"; an award for "the loss

235 Ibid, p. 802G

236 Op. cit. at p.309A

of services only a mother could provide"; and an award for "the loss of intangible benefits".

Although the origin of this type of award was an *"attempt by the courts to value the services of a mother … to a child over and above the commercial cost of replacing her"*[237] this type of award has now been extended to cover cases involving the loss of a spouse or partner. In the case of *Beesley v New Century Group*[238] Hamblen J stated, *"In principle there is no reason for differentiating between the position of children and spouses in connection with the availability of such awards"*[239].

As we shall see below, the case law demonstrates that over time claims for this type of award have been framed as an attempt to compensate two different types of loss:

a) A claim for pecuniary loss: the value of services provided by the deceased that are over and above those reflected in the commercial cost of replacing those services.

b) A claim for non-pecuniary loss: a claim solely for the "love and affection" provided by the deceased that has been lost.

This type of award is separate from an award for bereavement. The bereavement award is a statutory award. It is a set amount determined by statute which is currently £12,980 for deaths after the 1st of April 2013 and £15,120 for deaths after the 1st May 2020. The bereavement award is discussed in detail at chapter fourteen of this book.

---

237 Per Mackay J Fleet v Fleet EWHC 3166 (QB) para 24

238 [2008] EWHC 3033 (QB)

239 Ibid, para 83

13.4 THE LEVEL OF THE AWARD

The amount awarded is not set at a particular level but is at the individual judge's discretion. The awards made under this heading are relatively modest. Reported cases show that awards generally range from £1,000 to £3,000[240]. The upper end of the bracket of awards seems to be around £5,000 at present. This may increase slightly in line with inflation.

In the case of *ATH & Anr v MS*[241] the Court of Appeal reduced awards made under the heading *"services only a mother can provide"* from £5000 and £7000 to £3,500 and £4,500 respectively. Kennedy LJ stated:

> *"The awards…of £5000 and £7000 are challenged by Mr Strachan on the basis that the conventional maximum award is about £5000, even where the dependant child is very young…Mr Lederman's response is that in other cases there was no evidence as to the value and quality of the services lost. In my judgment that is not a sufficient reason to abandon the bracket, and I would reduce the award…"*[242]

13.5 SUCCESSFUL CLAIMS BASED ON A PECUNIARY LOSS

The Fatal Accidents Act is concerned almost entirely with pecuniary loss; that is a loss that can be valued in pounds and pence. The only exception to this is the bereavement award. The bereavement award is an attempt (some would say a poor one) to compensate the claimant for the non-pecuniary loss of the grief and emotional trauma caused by bereavement.

Within this framework there remains ample scope for the Court to make a "Regan v Williamson" type of award. When the Court makes this type

---

240 £1,000 was awarded in the case of Mehmet Op. cit; £3,000 was awarded in the case of Knauer Op cit.

241 [2002] EWCA Civ 792

242 Ibid at para 38

of award they are doing so as an estimation of an additional pecuniary loss that cannot be adequately compensated for solely by the services dependency claim.

In the case of *Beesley* Hamblen J explained:

> *"In my judgment the principle of making awards for loss of intangible benefits is now well established…It reflects the fact that services may be provided by a mother, wife, father or husband over and above that which may be provided by a paid replacement."*[243]

In the case of *Grant v Secretary of State for Transport*[244], after a comprehensive review of the case law, Martin Chamberlin QC (sitting as a Deputy High Court Judge) concluded:

> *"First, aside for the award for bereavement, there can be no claim under the 1976 Act for non-pecuniary loss…*
>
> *Second the courts have sometimes recognised that the claimant may suffer a pecuniary loss as a result of the death of a relative that was not adequately compensated by an award for services dependency. A pecuniary loss, for these purposes, means a loss that is conceptually capable of being valued in money or money's worth…Awards made on this basis do not offend the principle that, bereavement apart, compensation is available for pecuniary loss only. They are simply an attempt to capture more accurately the pecuniary value of the deceased's services…"*

There are numerous examples where a "Regan v Williamson" award has been made on the basis that there is a modest additional pecuniary benefit that cannot be compensated solely by the damages calculated for services dependency. The Courts have identified the additional pecuniary benefit provided by the deceased in: the special quality of care provided by a

243 Op. cit. at para 83

244 [2017] EWHC 1663 (QB)

parent[245]; providing higher quality care and assistance to the elderly and the disabled[246] and value in the convenience of not having to arrange for various services to be performed commercially[247]. In all these situations the Courts have made modest "Regan v Williamson" type awards accordingly.

13.6 UNSUCCESSFUL CLAIMS BASED ON PECUNIARY LOSS

Sometimes the Court concludes that it is unnecessary to award an additional sum after the award for services dependency has been calculated and declines to make a "Regan v Williamson" type award. In the case of *Mosson v Spousal (London) Ltd*[248] Garnham J (having observed that the legal basis for making such awards was unclear) analysed whether there had been an additional pecuniary loss. He determined that there had not been and declined to make such an award. He also concluded that there was not any proper legal basis for this type of award at all. He stated:

> *"I take on board the fact that the making of awards of this sort has become increasingly commonplace. However I regret to say that, for two reasons, I find myself in disagreement with the conclusions of the*

245 Regan Op. cit. Mehmet v Perry [1977] 2 All E.R. 529; Corbett v Barking Havering and Brentwood Health Authority [1992] 2 QB 408; Johnson v British Midland Airways Ltd [1996] PIQR Q8. See chapter 8.5.4 for a further discussion of awards made on this basis.

246 Fleet v Fleet Op. Cit; Also (arguably) Devoy v Doxford [2009] EWHC 159 (QB)

247 Grant Op. cit; Beesley Op. cit; Wolstenholme v Leach's of Sunderhill Ltd [2016] EWHC 588 (QB); Blake v Mad Max Limited [2018] EWHC 2134

248 [2016] EWHC 53 (QB)

> *other judges of this Court to whom I have referred. I can see no proper jurisprudential foundation for this claim[249].*"

In summary, Garnham J went on to state that the first reason he would not make such an award was because there can be no precise equivalence in money terms of every loss that flows from an injury or a death; the court had to do its best to calculate the pecuniary loss and had done so in the present case. Secondly, he stated that any claim that is not for a pecuniary loss was the type of loss that the statutory bereavement award was intended to cover[250].

In the case of *Magill v Panel Systems (DB) Ltd*[251] HHJ Gosnell (sitting as a High Court Judge) observed that *"such claims had become commonplace"* but found that on the facts of the case there could be no additional pecuniary loss which was capable of compensation. He declined to make an award for the loss of a partner's care and attention in the emotional (non-pecuniary) sense. He concluded:

> *"I have no doubt that the Claimant has lost the care stated and attention of the deceased in the emotional sense and the loss of that cannot be minimised but it does not sound in additional damages because this is exactly the loss that the bereavement award (modest though it is) is intended to compensate for."*[252]

13.7 SUCCESSFUL CLAIMS BASED ON NON-PECUNIARY LOSS

As we have seen, with the exception of the bereavement award, as Edmund-Davies LJ observed, *"it is undoubtedly the case that damages*

249 Ibid at para 71

250 Ibid at paras 72-75

251 [2017] EWHC 1517 (QB)

252 Ibid at para 65

under the fatal accidents act can only be awarded in respect of pecuniary loss and not as a solatium for injured feelings"[253].

Nevertheless, occasionally claims continue to be made for the "loss of love and affection" of the deceased both in the context of deceased spouses and partners and of deceased parents. Following the analysis set out in the cases above (and in particular in the case of *Grant*) the reader could be forgiven for expecting that these claims would fail. However, Courts do sometimes make awards on this basis.

In the case of *CC v TD*[254] HHJ Freedman (sitting as a High Court Judge) stated:

> *"…a claim for loss of intangible benefits on behalf of the children falls into an entirely different category and is to be distinguished from the type of claim made in Mosson…I am satisfied that the line of cases starting with Hay in 1975 permit the Court to make an award for loss of intangible benefits where children have been denied the benefit of love and affection which their father would otherwise have bestowed upon them. Experience suggests that such awards are commonplace"*[255]

HHJ went on to award £5,000 for each child dependant.

In addition to awards made in Court, the author has experience of claims settling out of court where sums of up to £4,000 have been allowed for "loss of love and affection" where it is clear the sum contended for does not relate to a pecuniary loss.

---

253 See above at 13.2

254 [2018] EWHC 1240 (QB)

255 Ibid paragraphs 56-57

13.7 LIMITS ON THE AWARD

It seems clear that if a "Regan v Williamson" award is made it is confined to minor children. In the case of *Chouza*[256] a claim was made for "loss of intangible benefits" in the sum of £3000 for each of the adult sons of the deceased. Mr Justice Martin Spencer dismissed the claim for the adult sons and stated:

Although this head of loss has been extended to the spouses of the deceased, it has historically been confined to claims by minor children, that is, non-adults...the claim in respect of Alberto, David and Lucas appears to be a significant extension to the class of claimants to which this head of loss traditionally applies and it appears to be put on a significantly wider basis...In my judgment, the law does not extend this far and this head of loss is to be confined to spouses and minor children of the deceased[257].

Although this author has experience of awards being agreed in settlements for adult children, and there are instances of courts making awards on occasion, the analysis in *Chouza* must be correct. In the case of *ATH & Anr v MS*[258]at first instance an award had been made to an adult child (19 years old). However, only the level of this award was challenged on appeal, not the fact that it had been made at all[259]. The issue of whether an award can be made to an adult child was not examined by the Court of appeal. In that case the Court of appeal did state that the sum of £5,000 was the "conventional maximum"[260] and reduced two of the awards from £5,000 and £7,000 to £3,500 and £4,000 respectively.

256 Chouza v Martins [2021] EWHC 1669 (QB)

257 Ibid, at paras 87-88

258 [2002] EWCA Civ 792

259 Ibid at para 38

260 Ibid at para 38

13.8 SUMMARY

In summary:

a) This type of award is based on the principle derived from the case of *Regan v Willamson.*

b) It is separate from the bereavement award.

c) It is awarded to minor children and spouses.

d) The amounts awarded are modest and tend to range from £1,000 to £3,000 although damages of up to £5,000 have been made.

e) Different Judges take different approaches to this type of award, and it is not certain that a court will make such an award.

f) The court frequently makes this type of award as an estimation of an additional pecuniary loss that cannot be adequately compensated for solely by the services dependency claim.

g) Sometimes the court makes this type of award to compensate for the non-pecuniary loss of lost love and affection although the legal basis for such an award is, at best, unclear.

CHAPTER FOURTEEN

THE BEREAVEMENT AWARD

14.1 INTRODUCTION

This chapter considers:

a) The historical development of the statutory award for bereavement;

b) The limited class of relatives who can claim it;

c) The level of the award and the effect of the Damages for Bereavement (Variation of Sum) (England and Wales) Order 2020;

d) The case of Smith v Lancashire Teaching Hospitals NHS Foundation Trust & Ors[261].

14.2 HISTORICAL DEVELOPMENT

Although in Scottish law it has long been possible to make awards in damages for "loss of society" it was not until the Administration of Justice Act 1982 inserted S1A into the Fatal Accidents Act 1976 that the Courts of England and Wales could make a stand alone award for

261 [2017] EWCA Civ 1916

bereavement[262]. The bereavement award is entirely statutory. It remains the position that there is no facility at common law to award damages for *"the normal emotions of grief, sorrow or distress on the death of a loved one"*[263].

14.3 THOSE WHO CAN CLAIM

Section 1A(2) of the Fatal Accidents Act 1976 sets out the (very) limited class of relatives who are entitled to claim a bereavement award.

> *A claim for damages for bereavement shall only be for the benefit—*
>
> *(a)of the wife or husband [or civil partner] of the deceased;*
>
> *(aa)of the cohabiting partner of the deceased; and*
>
> *(b)where the deceased was a minor who was never married [or a civil partner]—*
>
> *(i)of his parents, if he was legitimate; and*
>
> *(ii)of his mother, if he was illegitimate.*
>
> *[(2A)In subsection (2) "cohabiting partner" means any person who—*
>
> *(a)was living with the deceased in the same household immediately before the date of the death; and*
>
> *(b)had been living with the deceased in the same household for at least two years before that date; and*

---

262 See the case of Haggerty-Garton v ICI Ltd [2021] EWHC 2924 (QB) for an example of how the Scottish system approaches this head of loss. The award returned is considerably higher.

263 Kerby v Redbridge HA [1994] P.I.Q.R Q1

(c)was living during the whole of that period as the wife or husband or civil partner of the deceased.]

These are the only classes of individuals entitled to the bereavement award. Unlike with awards for financial dependency there is no requirement for those who claim the award to prove a reasonable expectation of pecuniary benefit. Fulfilling the statutory entitlement is the only qualifying factor necessary to claim the award.

There is no entitlement for a bereavement award for children although children can advance an award for the special quality of their parents' care that has been lost. This type of award is called a Regan v Williamson award and is discussed in detail at chapters eight and thirteen[264].

The limited list of those who are entitled to claim the bereavement award has caused controversy. There is still no entitlement for an award for bereavement for the parents of a child who is aged 18 or over at its death[265] or for an unmarried father of a child. Only the mother of an illegitimate child can claim the bereavement award. General criticisms of the bereavement award are discussed in more detail below.

The Fatal Accidents Act 1976 (Remedial) Order 2020 (finally) came into force on the on 6th October 2020. This order resolves the incompatibility of S1A of the Act with Section 4 of the Human Rights Act as first identified by the Court of Appeal as long ago as 2016 in the case of *Smith v Lancashire Teaching Hospitals NHS Trust & Ors*[266]. The FAA '76 now

264 See chapter 8.5.4

265 See Doleman v Deakin CA (1990) Times 30th January where the deceased was less than a month over the 18 year age limit and a bereavement award was not allowed by the court.

266 [2016] EWHC 2208 (QB)

permits cohabitees who have been living together for 2 years to claim the bereavement payment[267].

14.5 THE LEVEL OF THE AWARD

The level of the award is varied periodically by statutory instrument[268]. The latest variation was made by the Damages for Bereavement (Variation of Sum) (England and Wales) Order 2020. This Order came into force on 1st May 2020. This order sets the level of the bereavement award at £15,120 in relation to deaths after the 1st May 2020. The level of the bereavement award is £12,980[269] for deaths after the 1st April 2013 and before the 1st May 2020.

Previously the award was £10,000 for deaths post the 1st of April 2002 and £11,800 for deaths after the 1st January 2009.

The court makes one award for bereavement which is then split between all entitled parties. So where two parents claim the bereavement award it is split equally between them[270]. The Fatal Accidents Act 1976 (Remedial) Order 2020 specifies that where both a cohabitee and a spouse is eligible for the bereavement award it should divided equally between them[271].

---

267 For a full discussion of the case of *Smith* see the 2nd edition of this work at chapter 14

268 See: The Damages for Bereavement (Variation of Sum) (England and Wales) Order 2013 (S.I. 2013/510)

269 The increase of 10% has been made because of the Court of Appeal's ruling in the case of Simmons v Castle [2013] 1 W.L.R. 1239 CA

270 See S1(A) 4 of the Fatal Accidents Act 1976

271 See Article 2(4) of the Fatal Accidents 1976 (Remedial) Order

14.6 CRITICISM OF THE CURRENT APPROACH

Both the level of the bereavement award and the limited class of individuals who are entitled to claim it have come in for a great deal of criticism from many quarters.

14.6.1 THE AMOUNT

Although the amount of the award has now been slightly increased, almost all commentators make the point that it is derisory. The Law Commission, as long ago as 1999, suggested that an upper limit of £30,000 be placed on the award[272].

The approach north of the border remains markedly different to the approach in the English and Welsh courts and this perhaps adds to the sense of perceived unfairness. In Scotland, awards for "loss of society" can be much higher than the £15,120 limit and awards are made outside of the restrictive category of entitled individuals set by the Fatal Accidents Act 1976[273].

It may well be that, by leaving the determination of the level of the award to the courts, a fairer overall approach would be achieved. However, short of allowing the courts to make awards of very large sums of money it is difficult to see what sum of money can ever "fairly" compensate a grieving relative for the loss of their loved one.

---

272 The Law Commission (Law Com no 263) Claims for Wrongful Death November 1999 see 6.8

273 See: Bellington v Todd [2011] CSOH 74 and Ryder v Highland Council [2013] CSOH 95 and Haggerty-Garton v ICI Ltd [2021] EWHC 2924 (QB).

14.6.2 THE LIMITED CLASS OF INDIVIDUALS ENTITLED

In 1999 the Law Commission also criticised the limited class of individuals who are entitled to a bereavement award. In their report on claims for wrongful death they pointed out that:

> *...finite lists inevitably exclude deserving claimants, a problem avoided if the list were replaced or extended by a general class of persons entitled to sue...* [274]

In 2007, following a consultation, a draft bill was published to amend the class of persons entitled to a bereavement award to include cohabitees of over 2 years and children of the deceased who were under 18 years at the time of death[275]. However, the incoming government in 2010 decided not to pass the bill. No coherent reason was given[276]. It seems that despite continued and valid criticism of the law surrounding bereavement payments there is no sign of change in the foreseeable future.

14.7 SUMMARY

In summary:

a) Section 1A(2) of the Fatal Accidents Act 1976 sets out the (very) limited class of relatives who are entitled to claim a bereavement award;

---

274 The Law Commission (Law Com No 263) Claims for Wrongful Death paragraph 6.9 page 92

275 "Civil Law Reform: a Draft Bill" (Cm. 7773, December 2009)

276 Jonathan Djanogly MP Parliamentary Under-Secretary of State for Justice stated at the time: “"In the present financial situation we need to focus our resources on delivering our key priorities."

b) Only those individuals listed in the Act are entitled to the bereavement award;

c) S1A was amended (in October 2020) by the Fatal Accidents Act 1976 (Remedial) Order 2020 to allow cohabitees of more than 2 years to claim the bereavement award.

d) The level of the award is varied periodically by statutory instrument[277]. It is currently set at £15,120[278] for deaths after the 1st May 2020.

e) Both the level of the bereavement award and the limited class of individuals who are entitled to claim it have come in for a great deal of criticism from many quarters.

---

277 See: The Damages for Bereavement (Variation of Sum) (England and Wales) Order 2013 (S.I. 2013/510)

278 The increase of 10% has been made because of the Court of Appeal's ruling in the case of Simmons v Castle [2013] 1 W.L.R. 1239 CA

CHAPTER FIFTEEN

FUNERAL EXPENSES

15.1 INTRODUCTION

In this chapter the recoverability of funeral expenses under the Fatal Accidents Act 1976 and the Law Reform (Miscellaneous Provisions) Act 1934 is examined. The types of expense that the courts allow and disallow are identified. The issue of claiming funeral expenses before death is discussed.

15.2 THE STATUTORY BASIS

Funeral expenses are recoverable by dependants under both the Fatal Accidents Act 1976 and the Law Reform (Miscellaneous Provisions) Act 1934.

The recovery of funeral expenses is a stand-alone right provided for by section 3(5) of the Fatal Accidents Act 1976. Section 3(5) states:

> *If the dependants have incurred funeral expenses in respect of the deceased, damages may be awarded in respect of those expenses.*

To qualify as a dependant for the purposes of section 3(5) an individual must fulfil the statutory definition of a dependant as set out in section 1(3) of the Act. It is not necessary for the purposes of a claim for funeral expenses under section 3(5) to demonstrate a reasonable expectation of pecuniary benefit from the deceased. Accordingly where a claim for dependency fails, a claim for funeral expenses can still succeed[279]. Dependants can recover the expenses of the deceased's funeral even if there has not been a grant of probate made.

Funeral expenses are also recoverable by the estate of the deceased under the section 1(2)(c) of the Law Reform (Miscellaneous Provisions) Act 1934.

In circumstances where a dependant's actions have contributed to the deceased's death, it is better to make a claim for funeral expenses under the Law Reform (Miscellaneous Provisions) Act 1934. This is because under the Law Reform (Miscellaneous Provisions) Act 1934 no reduction is made to account for the fact that the negligence of the dependant contributed to the death. Under the Fatal Accidents Act 1976 a reduction is made to the damages awarded to reflect the negligence of the dependant[280].

15.3 WHAT CAN BE RECOVERED

There is no statutory definition of what constitutes a recoverable funeral expense under either Act. To be recoverable, funeral expenses must be reasonable in all the circumstances including the deceased's station in life, creed and racial origin[281]. The open-ended nature of this test has meant that decisions of the Court vary on what is allowed as a recoverable expense. It is clear that decisions in this area are particularly fact-sensitive.

279 Stanton v Ewart F Youldon Ltd [1960] 1 WLR 543, 545; Burns v Edman [1970] 2 QB 541, 546

280 Mullholland v McCrea [1961] NI 135

281 Gammell v Wilson [1982] AC 27

15.3.1 HEADSTONES AND MEMORIALS

Generally, it seems that courts will allow the cost of a headstone to mark the grave but not the cost of a memorial. The distinction between a headstone to mark the grave and a memorial can be traced back to the case of *Hart v Griffiths-Jones*[282] and the distinction was confirmed in later cases[283]. In the case of *Mosson v Spousal (London) Ltd* [284] Mr Justice Garnham cited the case of *Gammell v Wilson*[285] as authority for the fact that a headstone that marks the grave is a legitimate expense, but the cost of a memorial is not. In that case the cost of a memorial bench was not allowed.

There have been some exceptions to this rule. A claim for a memorial did apparently succeed in the unreported case of *Kegworth v British Midland Airways*[286]. In the unusual case of *St George v Turner*[287] the court allowed a claim of over £50,000 under the Law Reform (Miscellaneous Provisions) Act 1934 for expenses which included the cost of building a Buddhist family altar in Japan. This author is not alone in considering the case of *St George* to be incorrectly decided. It is also difficult to reconcile the decision in *Kegworth* and *St George* with the decisions in *Mosson*, *Knauer* and *Gammell*. It is submitted that the approach recently confirmed in *Mosson* is the correct approach.

282 [1948] 2 All E.R. 729

283 See also the case of Stanton v Ewart F Youldon Ltd [1960] 1 WLR 543 and Gammell op cit

284 [2016] EWHC 53 (QB)

285 [1982] AC 27

286 (Unreported) see Kemp & Kemp vol 1 paragraph 20-022

287 [2003] CLY 936

15.3.2 WAKES

Generally, the cost of a wake will not be allowed on assessment by the court. The cost of a wake was not allowed in the case of *Mosson* with Mr Justice Garnham relying on the decision in *Gammell* as confirmed in the case of *Knauer v Ministry of Justice*[288]. Mr Justice Garnham stated:

> *Bean J (as he then was) pointed out in Knauer v Ministry of Justice that, in the first instance decision in Gammell v Wilson, Mr Bennet Hytener QC, sitting as a deputy judge, disallowed the costs of a wake. As Bean J held "Mr Hytener's decision has been regarded as good law ever since". He was not prepared to depart from it and nor am I.*[289]

The cost of funeral clothes and the cost of (what was on any view) an elaborate wake were not allowed in the case of *Quainoo v Brent & Harrow Health Authority*[290]. The cost of a wake was also not allowed in the case of *Jones v Royal Devon & Exeter NHS Foundation Trust*[291] .

The cost of a wake was not allowed in the case of *Grant*[292] on the basis that *"Receptions are not always held after a funeral. When they are held, there is no invariable practice of providing refreshments. This makes it difficult to suppose that Parliament intended to include them within "funeral*

288 [2014] EWHC 2553 (QB)

289 [2016] EWHC 53 (QB) at para 49

290 (1982) 132 NLJ 1100. This unusual case concerned the death of a member of the Ghanaian Royal family. While the costs associated with wake were disallowed the costs of cars for the funeral procession in Ghana and also the cost of transporting the body to Ghana were allowed.

291 [2008] EWHC 558 QB

292 [2017] EWHC 1663 (QB)

expenses"[293] Most recently the cost of a wake was not allowed in the case of *Blake v Mad Max Ltd.*[294]

In the case of *St George* the considerable cost of a memorial day and an anniversary reception were both allowed. However, as discussed above, this case must surely be wrongly decided in light of the other authorities in this area. There are instances where very modest claims for expenses which are strictly for a wake or reception have succeeded at first instance and this author has had some success in settling modest claims out of court for the costs associated with a wake[295].

15.3.3 PROBATE FEES

It seems unlikely that, on a strict analysis, the costs associated with probate can be considered a funeral expense recoverable as damages. While it can be argued that the costs associated with probate should be recovered as damages because the sole reason for incurring those costs was to bring the action, it cannot be said that this argument is likely to succeed. In the case of *Mosson*[296] a claim for the costs associated with probate under the Law Reform (Miscellaneous Provisions) Act 1934 was refused as there was no reference to probate costs in the 1934 Act. In the case of *Read v Harries*[297] Morland J stated:

> *My provisional view is that the probate costs are not recoverable either as a head of damages or as costs. The grant of probate was not*

293 Ibid para 55

294 [2018] EWHC 2134 (QB)

295 Smith v Marchioness/ Bowbelle (27 January 1993) The Times

296 [2016] EWHC 53 (QB)

297 Read v Harries [1995] PIQR Q 25

> *obtained for the purposes of bringing this action in which the writ was not issued until September 13, 1989.*

The sums involved in probate fees are often modest in the scheme of the claim as a whole and, perhaps for this reason, defendants are often willing to pay the probate fees in cases that settle outside of court. Despite the comments of Morland J in *Read* this author has had some success with recovering the cost of probate fees as a cost at the conclusion of litigation.

15.3.4 BROADER CLAIMS

The term "funeral expenses" is capable of being given a relatively generous interpretation by the courts. For example, a claim for the cost of embalming the deceased has succeeded[298]. In the case of *Schneider v Eisovitch*[299] the court allowed a claim for expenses of friends of the deceased who arranged for the return of the body of the deceased from France. In the case of *Quainoo*[300] the cost of flying the deceased's coffin back to Ghana was allowed. While claims for travel connected to the funeral are in principle permitted, they are fact sensitive and must still be shown to be reasonable in all the circumstances. For example, in the case of *Thompson v Neilly*[301] the cost of flights to the USA to settle the deceased's affairs including arrangements for attending the funeral was not allowed.

298 Hart v Griffiths- Jones op.cit.

299 [1960] 2 QB 430

300 (1982) 132 NLJ 1100

301 1973 S.L.T. 53

15.4 CLAIMS BEFORE DEATH

There is some disagreement at judicial level as to whether a claim can be made for funeral expenses under the Law Reform (Miscellaneous Provisions) Act 1934 before the individual's death. It is submitted that the correct approach is that they cannot.

In the case of *Bateman v Hydro Agri (UK) ltd*[302] Anthony Temple QC, sitting as a deputy High Court judge allowed such a claim. However, in the case of *Watson v Cakebread*[303] Satindar Hunjan QC, also sitting as a deputy High Court judge, denied a claim for funeral expenses before death. He pointed out that:

> *Following the claimant's submissions would have the curious consequence that a "living" claimant could litigate in respect of all the anticipated gains and losses of his estate as if he were acting on behalf of his estate while alive.*

It is hard to refute the logic in the decision in *Watson* and accordingly it is suggested that this is the correct approach.

15.5 SUMMARY

In summary:

a) Funeral expenses can be claimed under the Fatal Accidents Act 1976 and the Law Reform (Miscellaneous Provisions) Act 1934;

b) There is no statutory definition of funeral expenses;

---

302 Unreported see: Kemp & Kemp vol 1 29-063

303 [2010] EWHC 1695

c) Claims for funeral expenses must be reasonable in all the circumstances including the deceased's station in life, creed and racial origin;

d) Claims for headstones are allowed;

e) Claims for memorials are generally not allowed;

f) Claims for the cost of a wake are generally not allowed;

g) Claims for broader expenses connected to the funeral (such as international travel) are permissible but it must still be demonstrated that such claims are reasonable in all the circumstances;

h) It is unlikely that the court will permit a claim for funeral expenses whilst the claimant is still alive.

CHAPTER SIXTEEN

CLAIMS FOR PAIN, SUFFERING AND LOSS OF AMENITY AND OTHER LOSSES OF THE DECEASED BEFORE DEATH UNDER THE LAW REFORM (MISCELLANEOUS PROVISIONS) ACT 1934

16.1 INTRODUCTION

The Law Reform (Miscellaneous Provisions) Act 1934 enables claims by the deceased's estate for:

a) Funeral expenses and;

b) Claims for pain, suffering and loss of amenity and other losses suffered by the deceased before death.

Funeral expenses can also be recovered under the Fatal Accidents Act 1976. The issue of funeral expenses has been discussed in detail at chapter fifteen. In this chapter we consider claims brought by the estate for pain, suffering and loss of amenity and other losses suffered by the deceased before death.

16.2 RIGHT OF ACTION

Claims for the losses that the deceased suffered before death can only be brought by the estate of the deceased by virtue of the Law Reform

(Miscellaneous Provisions) Act 1934. This type of claim cannot be brought by dependants as a claim under the Fatal Accidents Act 1976 can. If the claim is brought by an administrator before a grant of probate has been obtained, then the proceedings are a nullity and stand to be struck out. The CPR cannot operate to save a claim in these circumstances[304].

If the claim is brought by an executor before a grant of probate is obtained, then it is not a nullity. The cause of action to bring the claim automatically vests in the executor at the moment of death[305]. The grant of probate is proof of the executor's standing to bring the claim and will need to be produced during the claim in any event.

16.3 MATTERS WHICH CANNOT BE RECOVERED UNDER THE LAW REFORM (MISCELLANEOUS PROVISIONS) ACT 1934

16.3.1 PROSPECTIVE LOSS OF INCOME

Claims by the estate under the Law Reform (Miscellaneous Provisions) Act 1934 are concerned with the pain, suffering, loss of amenity and other losses that the deceased suffered between the injury or event which caused the death and the deceased's death. Accordingly, it is not possible to recover claims for prospective loss of income of the deceased under the Law Reform (Miscellaneous Provisions) Act 1934 and it has not been possible to do this for some time.

304 Haastrup -v- Okorie [2016] EWHC 12 (Ch); Kimathi & Ors -v- The Foreign & Commonwealth Office [2016] EWHC

305 Ibid at paras 20 -22; Ingall v Moran [1944] KB 160 at page 164

In the past it was possible for the estate to make a claim for prospective earnings of the deceased[306]. This position was unsatisfactory as it led to the possibility of double recovery. Double recovery could occur because the tortfeasor might have to pay damages in relation to the prospective earnings of the deceased to the estate and then also to the dependants, who might be different individuals. As with many unsatisfactory aspects of the law pertaining to claims for wrongful death, legislation was surprisingly slow to correct this position. After a delay of almost two years section 4 of the Administration of Justice Act 1982 inserted section 1(2)(a) into the Law Reform (Miscellaneous Provisions) Act 1934 which stated:

> *Where a cause of action survives as aforesaid for the benefit of the estate of a deceased person, the damages recoverable for the benefit of the estate of that person—*
>
> *a) shall not include—*
>
> *i. any exemplary damages;*
>
> *ii. any damages for loss of income in respect of any period after that person's death;*

Since this amendment any claim for loss of income resulting from an individual's death cannot be claimed under the Law Reform (Miscellaneous Provisions) Act 1934 and is now properly pursued under the Fatal Accidents Act 1982. Chapters six, seven, eight, nine and ten discuss how to advance this type of claim in detail.

306 This was as a result of the decision in Pickett v Railway Engineering Op. cit. as confirmed in the case of Gammell v Wilson Op. cit.

16.3.2 OTHER PROSPECTIVE LOSSES

As a matter of logic, there can be no claim by the estate for any other prospective losses under the Law Reform (Miscellaneous Provisions) Act 1934. When the individual has died any prospect of any further losses has been removed. There can be no claim by the estate for pain and suffering of the deceased which in fact the deceased had not experienced.

In reality this is an area that is unlikely to trouble practitioners. This area only merits any discussion at all because of the fact that general damages are also recovered for "loss of amenity"[307] and the conclusions of the House of Lords regarding the nature of "loss of amenity" as a head of loss in the case of *West v Shephard*[308]. In that case the House of Lords allowed a substantial award for loss of amenity to an unconscious claimant. Despite the fact that the claimant was not, and could never be, aware of his loss of amenity, the House of Lords held by a bare majority that the claimant's ignorance of the loss suffered was no ground for reducing the damages. This gave "loss of amenity" an objective status: the claimant could recover damages for loss of amenity even though he was not subjectively aware of losing any amenity. Applying the (slightly torturous) logic in *West v Shephard* it seems at least technically possible for the estate of the deceased to pursue a claim for the prospective loss of amenity the deceased has suffered even though, by his death, he was unaware of this.

In reality this is surely not a claim which can logically succeed, regardless of the decision in *West*. It cannot possibly be correct that the estate of the deceased can be entitled to damages for a period of loss of amenity that

307 The inclusion of the term "loss of amenities" as a distinct from pain and suffering starts to occur in the 1950's. See: Manley v Rugby Portland Cement Co (1951) CA No 286, Shearman v Folland [1950] 2 K.B. 43 CA

308 [1964] A.C. 326

extends beyond the deceased's death. No such claim has ever been advanced as far as case law relates.

16.4 EXEMPLARY AND AGGRAVATED DAMAGES

As we have seen above, exemplary damages are expressly excluded under S1 (2) (a) of the Law Reform (Miscellaneous Provisions) Act 1934. Aggravated damages are not excluded by the Law Reform (Miscellaneous Provisions) Act 1934.

A full discussion of the (much debated) relationship between exemplary and aggravated damages is beyond the scope of this book[309]. There follows a basic outline of the principles.

16.4.1 EXEMPLARY DAMAGES

Exemplary damages are punitive. Awards for exemplary damages are very rare. They are awarded when the defendant's conduct is so bad it merits punishment. Following the case of *Rookes v Barnard*[310] they can now only be awarded in three categories:

a) Cases where there has been oppressive, arbitrary or unconstitutional conduct by servants or agents of the government;

b) Cases where the Defendant's conduct has been calculated to make a profit which may exceed the compensation payable;

c) Where expressly provided for by statute.

309 For a full discussion see: The Law Commission Aggravated, Exemplary and Restitutionary Damages

310 [1964] A.C 1129

16.4.2 AGGRAVATED DAMAGES

Aggravated damages are compensatory in nature. Awards for aggravated damages are very rare. They are awarded to compensate the claimant for exceptional "injury to feelings including indignity, mental suffering, humiliation and distress as well as anger or indignation"[311]. They are most commonly awarded in cases where an assault has occurred. In the case of *Richardson v Howie*[312] the Court of Appeal stated that even in cases involving assault, aggravated damages should only be awarded in "a wholly exceptional case".

16.5 MATTERS WHICH CAN BE RECOVERED UNDER THE LAW REFORM (MISCELLANEOUS PROVISIONS) ACT 1934

16.5.1 PAIN, SUFFERING AND LOSS OF AMENITY BEFORE DEATH

Claims for the period of pain, suffering and loss of amenity that the deceased suffered between injury and death must be proved on the balance of probabilities, via evidence in the usual fashion.

The case of *Kadir v Mistry*[313] sets out a summary of the principles to be applied when assessing awards of damages for pain, suffering and loss of amenity prior to death. Lord Justice Laws stated:

> *It is in my judgment important to bear in mind on this part of the case that there are no special rules for the assessment of general damages for pain and suffering in a 1934 Act case compared with the case of a living claimant, save only the caveat in the Act which allows damages for mental anguish occasioned by the apprehension of an*

311 [2005] P.I.Q.R Q3 CA

312 Ibid

313 [2014] EWCA Civ 1177

> *early death. This part of the case requires the court to undertake what to my mind is a wholly conventional exercise: what elements of pain and suffering as a matter of causation had been occasioned to the deceased by the respondent's negligence?*[314]

In *Kadir* the Court of Appeal upheld the decision at first instance that there should be no award for pain, suffering and loss of amenity because there was no evidence that the level of pain and suffering and loss of amenity would be any different had the defendant not been negligent. The Court of Appeal reversed the decision at first instance and allowed the sum of £3,500 for the mental anguish caused by the apprehension of an early death. Damages for the apprehension of an early death are discussed in detail below.

16.5.2 THE LEVEL OF DAMAGES FOR INJURIES RESULTING IN DEATH

The latest (17th) edition of the Judicial College Guidelines contains a section that offers guidance on the appropriate level of damages for injuries resulting in death. This will be the starting point for any assessment. It states:

> *Fatal accident claims sometimes include an element for pain, suffering and loss of amenity for the period between injury and death. In some circumstances the awards may be high, for example those relating to asbestos exposure or misdiagnosis of cancer. Others follow extensive periods of disability before death supervenes. In such cases reference should be made to the awards for the underlying injuries or condition, suitably adjusted to reflect the fact (if it be the case) that the claimant knows that death is approaching, and the period of suffering.*

314 Ibid at para 11

Yet there are many cases in which a serious injury is followed relatively quickly by death. Factors that inform the level of general damages include the nature and extent of the injury, the claimant's awareness of his or her impending death, the extent of pain and suffering, or, in cases where the claimant is unconscious for all or part of the period, loss of amenity. Care should be taken where death follows very shortly after an accident. In Hicks v Chief Constable of South Yorkshire Police [1992] 2 All ER 65 the House of Lords refused to award damages to two victims of the Hillsborough disaster who died from traumatic asphyxia. Both lost consciousness within a matter of seconds and died within five minutes. No other physical injuries were sustained before the fatal crushing injuries. The Court ruled that fear of impending death alone did not give rise to a cause of action which survived for the benefit of the victim's estate. In Chouza v Martins and others [2021] EWHC 1669 (QB) damages of £500 were awarded in a case where the deceased had an awareness of an impending collision for between one and five seconds but died instantly at the point of impact with the trial judge relying on fear and anguish in association with physical injury. The Hicks case was not cited to the judge and the decision may be per incuriam.

Under s.1(1)(a) of the Administration of Justice Act 1982 awards may be made for 'mental anguish' (even in the absence of psychiatric injury) caused by awareness of curtailment of life: see Kadir v Mistry [2014] EWCA Civ 1177.

Section (A) – Full Awareness

Severe burns and lung damage followed by full awareness for a short period and then fluctuating levels of consciousness for between four and five weeks, coupled with intrusive treatment or significant orthopaedic/physical injuries followed by death within a couple of weeks up to three months.

£15,300 to £29,060

(B) Followed by Unconsciousness

Severe burns and lung damage causing excruciating pain but followed by unconsciousness after three hours and death two weeks later.

£12,830 to £13,020

(C) Immediate Unconsciousness/Death after Six Weeks

Immediate unconsciousness after injury, and death occurring after six weeks

£4,590 to £5,360

(D) Immediate Unconsciousness/Death within One Week

Immediate unconsciousness, or unconsciousness following very shortly after injury, and death occurring within a week. Where the victim is conscious initially but dies from their injuries the same day an award towards the bottom of the range will be appropriate, subject to the comments at the start of this chapter relating to cases of near instant death.

£1,680 to £3,410

(E) Mental Anguish

Fear of impending death/reduction in expectation of life. For the parent of young children suffering such mental anguish for a period of around 3 months.

£5,700

16.5.3 DAMAGES FOR AWARENESS THAT EXPECTATION OF LIFE HAS BEEN REDUCED

When assessing general damages for the injury that caused death, the court will take into account any mental anguish caused by the knowledge that a claimant's life expectation has been reduced.

Section 1(1)(b) of the Administration of Justice Act 1982 specifically provides for this. It states:

> *b) if the injured person's expectation of life has been reduced by the injuries, the court, in assessing damages in respect of pain and suffering caused by the injuries, shall take account of any suffering caused or likely to be caused to him by awareness that his expectation of life has been so reduced.*

The figures set out in chapter one of the Judicial College Guidelines (see above) take into account this element of mental anguish. Chapter one (E) of the Judicial College Guidelines deals with the mental anguish in isolation and the figure of £5,700 is presumably based (at least in part) on the stand alone award for mental anguish made by the Court of Appeal in the case of *Kadir*[315].

If death is instantaneous, or virtually instantaneous, then (generally) no award will be made. In the case of *Hicks v Chief Constable of South Yorkshire*[316] the deceased died from traumatic asphyxia which had the effect that the deceased lost consciousness within seconds and died within 5 minutes thereafter. There was no proof before the court of any physical injury before death. The Court of Appeal held that there can be no damages for "pre-death terror" and that where death was instantaneous or virtually instantaneous "fear of impending death" could not of itself give rise to a cause of action that survived for the benefit of the deceased's estate.

However, in the (more recent) case of *Chouza v Martins*[317] damages of £500 were awarded where the evidence was that the deceased had an awareness of the impending collision of five seconds but died instantly at the point of impact. Mr Justice Martin Spencer stated at paragraph 20:

---

315 [2014] EWCA Civ 1177

316 [1992] All ER 65

317 [2021] EWHC 1669 (QB)

> *In my judgment, there is a distinction to be drawn between mere fear or anguish on its own and fear or anguish in association with physical injury. Although the deceased's death followed very quickly after the physical injury, nevertheless physical injury was sustained, and the expression "pain, suffering and loss of amenity" should be taken to include the fear and mental anguish which precedes physical injury. [...] In my judgment, the appropriate sum to be awarded is £500.*[318]

This aspect of the decision in *Chouza* has been criticised by some commentators. In the preamble to the Judicial College Guidelines[319] on injuries resulting in death it is suggested that the decision was made *per incuriam* because the case of Hicks was not cited to the Judge.

It may be that the difference between the two cases lies in the factual findings that preceded the application of the law. In the case of *Hicks* it was specifically found that there was no physical injury before death whereas in the case of *Chouza* Mr Justice Martin Spencer states "nevertheless physical injury was sustained."

16.6 OTHER HEADS OF LOSS

The estate of the deceased can make a claim for other losses the deceased sustained in the period between injury and death, such as:

a) Loss of earnings;

b) Damage to vehicles, clothing etc.;

c) Care and assistance (gratuitous or professional).

---

318 Ibid at para 20

319 See above chapter 16.5.2

The losses must be proved on the balance of probability, via evidence, in the usual fashion.

16.7 SUMMARY

In summary:

a) The Law Reform (Miscellaneous Provisions) Act 1934 enables claims by the deceased's estate for:

    1. Funeral expenses and;

    2. Claims for pain, suffering and loss of amenity and other losses suffered by the deceased before death.

b) Claims for the losses that the deceased suffered before death can only be brought by the estate of the deceased by virtue of the Law Reform (Miscellaneous Provisions) Act 1934;

c) It is not possible to recover claims for prospective loss of income of the deceased under the Law Reform (Miscellaneous Provisions) Act 1934;

d) Awards of exemplary damages are expressly excluded under S1 (2) (a) of the Law Reform (Miscellaneous Provisions) Act 1934;

e) Claims for the period of pain, suffering and loss of amenity that the deceased suffered between injury and death must be proved on the balance of probabilities, via evidence in the usual fashion;

f) The latest (17th) edition of the Judicial College Guidelines contains a section that offers guidance on the appropriate level of damages for injuries resulting in death. This will be the starting point for any assessment;

g) When assessing general damages for the injury that caused death, the court will take into account any mental anguish caused by the knowledge that a claimant's life expectation has been reduced;

h) If death is instantaneous, or virtually instantaneous, and there is no proof of physical injury, then generally no award will be made solely for "pre-death terror";

i) The estate of the deceased can make a claim for other losses the deceased sustained in the period between injury and death such as loss of earnings, care and assistance etc.

CHAPTER SEVENTEEN

CLAIMS UNDER THE CRIMINAL INJURIES COMPENSATION SCHEME

17.1 INTRODUCTION

The Criminal Injuries Compensation Authority (hereinafter "CICA") operates a statutory system for providing compensation to innocent victims of violent crime. The scheme covers the situation where the criminal act causes death. The current scheme is the 2012 Criminal Injuries Compensation Scheme (revised) (hereinafter "the Scheme"). The paragraphs of the scheme that relate to fatal cases can be found at sections 57 to 84.

The CICA scheme is often the dependant's only option for compensation where the defendant has no money and is not insured. The scheme is a self-contained statutory system and all of the principles pertaining to compensation are contained within it. The principles (both common law and statutory) that have been set out in this book in relation to claims under the Fatal Accidents Act 1976 and the Law Reform (Miscellaneous Provisions) act 1934 do not apply at all to claims under the CICA scheme. Awards under the CICA scheme are potentially more limited than awards made in a civil claim for damages. The total amount paid to the qualifying claimants and the deceased will not exceed £500,000[320].

320 See para 84 of the Scheme.

17.2 ELIGIBILITY

A "qualifying relative" may make a claim if their relative died as a direct result of sustaining an injury in circumstances falling within paragraph 4 or 5 of the Scheme. Paragraph 4 states a person may claim "*if they sustain a criminal injury which is directly attributable to their being a direct victim of a crime of violence committed in a relevant place*".

Paragraph 5 states a person may claim:

> "*if they sustain a criminal injury which is directly attributable to their taking an exceptional and justified risk for the purpose, in a relevant place, of:*
>
> *(a) apprehending an offender or suspected offender;*
>
> *(b) preventing a crime;*
>
> *(c) containing or remedying the consequences of a crime; or*
>
> *(d) assisting a constable who is acting for one or more of the purposes described in paragraphs (a) to (c).*"

Further guidance on what qualifies as a "violent crime" in the context of the Scheme can be found in appendix B of the Scheme. The definition of a "qualifying relative" is discussed below. In common with the broader operation of the scheme payments can be reduced or refused if the deceased or the qualifying relative bringing the claim had a criminal record.

17.3 WHEN MUST THE CLAIM BE BROUGHT

Claims under the CICA scheme must generally be brought within two years of the incident. Paragraph 87 of the scheme states:

> *Subject to paragraph 88, an application must be sent by the applicant so that it is received by the Authority as soon as reasonably practicable after the incident giving rise to the criminal injury to which it relates, and in any event within two years after the date of that incident.*

Paragraph 88 extends the time limit in respect of minors. It states:

> *(1) Where the applicant was a child under the age of 18 on the date of the incident giving rise to the criminal injury, the application must be sent by the applicant so that it is received by the Authority:*
>
> > *(a) in the case of an incident reported to the police before the applicant's 18th birthday, within the period ending on their 20th birthday; or*
> >
> > *(b) in the case of an incident reported to the police on or after the applicant's 18th birthday, within two years after the date of the first report to the police in respect of the incident.*
>
> *(2) An application will not be accepted under this paragraph unless a claims officer is satisfied that the evidence presented in support of the application means that it can be determined without further extensive enquiries by a claims officer.*

The two-year time limit can be extended due to "exceptional circumstances"[321]. This provision is interpreted strictly by the CICA.

17.4 THOSE WHO CAN CLAIM

Under the scheme a "qualifying relative" may make a claim. Section 59 of the scheme defines who is a qualifying relative. It states:

321 See para 89 of the 2012 Criminal Injuries Compensation Scheme

A qualifying relative is a person who at the time of the deceased's death was:

(a) the spouse or civil partner of the deceased, who was living with the deceased in the same household;

(b) the partner of the deceased (other than a spouse or civil partner), who was living with them in the same household and had done so for a continuous period of at least two years immediately before the date of the death;

(c) a person who would satisfy sub-paragraph (a) or (b) but who did not live with the deceased because of either person's ill-health or infirmity;

(d) the spouse or civil partner, or a former spouse or civil partner, of the deceased who was financially dependent on the deceased;

(e) a parent of the deceased; or

(f) a child of the deceased.

17.5 BEREAVEMENT PAYMENTS

Paragraphs 61 and 62 of the Scheme set out the sums paid for a bereavement payment. This is currently £11,000. Where there is more than one qualifying claimant of this award, this amount is reduced to £5,500. Under the Scheme former spouses or partners and "those estranged from the deceased at the time of their death" do not qualify for a bereavement payment[322].

322 See para 61 of the Scheme

17.6 CHILD'S PAYMENTS

If the qualifying relative was a child at the time of death and was dependent on the deceased for "parental services" then paragraphs 63 to 66 of the Scheme set out the principles in relation to "child's payments". The period which the child's payment covers runs from the date of death until the child's 18th birthday. Paragraph 65 of the Scheme sets out the amounts paid:

> *The amount of a child's payment is:*
>
> *(a) £2,000 for each year (pro rata for each part year) of the period to which the payment relates; and;*
>
> *(b) such additional amount in relation to any expenses suffered by the child as a direct result of the loss of parental services as a claims officer considers reasonable.*

Paragraph 66 of the Scheme explains that the payment will be made in a lump sum and reduced by way of applying an appropriate multiplier selected by the CICA.

17.7 DEPENDENCY PAYMENTS

Paragraphs 67 to 74 of the Scheme set out the principles in relation to dependency payments. For a dependency payment to be made the qualifying relative must also be "financially dependent" on the deceased or the deceased must have been the qualifying relative's main carer. A payment will not be made if the deceased's main source of income was from social security benefits.

The amount of the payment is calculated by "reference to each week in which one or more qualifying relatives is eligible for a dependency payment". Paragraphs 68 and 69 of the Scheme explain how the period of dependency is calculated. The principles set out there are straight forward.

Paragraph 71 goes on to explain:

> *The total amount payable in each of those weeks will be the weekly rate, at the date of determination, of statutory sick pay under section 157 of the Social Security Contributions and Benefits Act 1992. The weekly amount will be divided in equal shares between each qualifying relative who is eligible in any week. A qualifying relative eligible for part of a week will be treated as if eligible for the whole of that week.*

Again, this amount is paid as a lump sum and reduced by way of applying an appropriate multiplier selected by the CICA.

17.8 FUNERAL EXPENSES

Paragraphs 75 to 77 set out the principles in relation to payments for funeral expenses. This is the only head of damage that can be paid to the estate of the deceased regardless of whether they meet the test for being a "qualifying relative". The amount is set at an initial £2,500 with provision for up to a maximum of a further £2,500 of expenses if they were "reasonably incurred".

17.9.1 THE EFFECT OF OTHER CLAIMS

Any award made under the CICA scheme may be reduced if there has been another award of damages resulting from the death. Sometimes the effect of this reduction is to remove entirely any award under the CICA scheme.

Paragraph 85 (1) of the Scheme states:

(1) An award under this Scheme will be withheld or reduced if in respect of the criminal injury to which the award relates the applicant, whether in any part of the United Kingdom or elsewhere:

(a) receives or is awarded criminal injuries compensation or a similar payment;

(b) receives an order for damages from a civil court;

(c) agrees the settlement of a damages claim; or

(d) receives a compensation order or offer made during criminal proceedings.

(2) An award will be reduced by the amount of any payments listed in sub-paragraph (1), net of any benefits recoverable under the Social Security (Recovery of Benefits) Act 1997 or equivalent legislation (whether in any part of the United Kingdom or elsewhere).

The award under the CICA scheme is reduced by the amount of the payment or award made elsewhere[323].

A recent example of a case where this occurred is the case of R. (on the application of AXO) v First-tier Tribunal (Social Entitlement Chamber)[324]. In that case the Claimant appellant (AXO) had been awarded £5,500 in damages in a CICA claim for bereavement. Damages were also awarded in an ECHR claim for breach of art. 2 in the sum of £10,000. The Court of Appeal stated that the CICA bereavement award and the ECHR damages paid in settlement of the art. 2 claim were paid for the same thing, namely AXO's grief and mental suffering in consequence of her mother's death. Accordingly, CICA could seek repayment of the £5,500.

323 Net of recoverable benefits under the Social Security (Recovery of Benefits) Act 1997. See para 85(2) of the Scheme.

324 [2024] EWCA Civ 226

17.9.2 SECOND AWARDS

Paragraph 78 of the Scheme states that a second award can be made under the Scheme where an award has already been made under the scheme to the deceased in respect of the injury that caused his death. Any further compensation paid will be reduced by the amount already paid to the deceased.

17.9.3 DEATH FROM AN UNRELATED CAUSE

Paragraphs 80 to 84 of the Scheme cover the circumstances where the deceased was a victim of a violent crime and then died of an unrelated cause. A qualifying relative who was financially dependent on the deceased may claim the amount of any award under the Scheme and may also receive a payment for any loss of earnings and any "*special expenses incurred by the deceased as a direct result of the criminal injury*"[325]. If there has already been some payment under the Scheme, then the amount paid to the qualifying relative is reduced by the amount of the partial payment.

17.10 SUMMARY

In summary:

a) The Criminal Injuries Compensation Authority operates a statutory system for providing compensation to innocent victims of violent crime;

b) A "qualifying relative" may make a claim if their relative died as a direct result of sustaining an injury in circumstances falling within paragraph 4 or 5 of the Scheme;

325 See para 82 of the Scheme.

c) Section 59 of the Scheme defines who is a qualifying relative;

d) Claims under the CICA scheme must generally be brought within two years of the incident;

e) Paragraphs 61 and 62 of the Scheme set out the sums paid for a bereavement payment. This is currently £11,000;

f) Paragraphs 63 to 66 of the Scheme set out the principles in relation to "child's payments";

g) Paragraphs 67 to 74 of the Scheme set out the principles in relation to dependency payments. For a dependency payment to be made the qualifying relative must also be "financially dependent" on the deceased or the deceased must have been the qualifying relative's main carer;

h) Paragraphs 75 to 77 set out the principles in relation to payments for funeral expenses. This is the only head of damage that can be paid to the estate of the deceased regardless of whether they meet the test for being a "qualifying relative";

i) Any award made under the CICA scheme may be reduced if there has been another award of damages resulting from the death.

CHAPTER EIGHTEEN

HUMAN RIGHTS CLAIMS

18.1 INTRODUCTION

It remains to be seen whether any of the legal framework created by the Human Rights Act 1998 will be retained given the political developments of summer 2016. For the time being, the Human Rights Act 1998 remains a consideration for the practitioner where the death of the deceased was caused by a public authority.

The mechanism by which the ECHR conducts cases and awards damages is substantially different from that which operates in the United Kingdom. A full discussion of the system is beyond the scope of this book. What follows is a discussion of the main areas in which the Human Rights Act 1998 can impact on a claim for damages following a fatal accident.

18.2 ACTIONS UNDER ARTICLE 2 – THE RIGHT TO LIFE

Article 2 of the Human Rights Act 1998 states:

> *1. Everyone's right to life shall be protected by law. No one shall be deprived of his life intentionally save in the execution of a sentence of a court following his conviction of a crime for which this penalty is provided by law.*
>
> *2. Deprivation of life shall not be regarded as inflicted in contravention of this Article when it results from the use of force which is no more than absolutely necessary:*

> *(a) in defence of any person from unlawful violence;*
>
> *(b) in order to effect a lawful arrest or to prevent the escape of a person lawfully detained;*
>
> *(c) in action lawfully taken for the purpose of quelling a riot or insurrection.*

Under the Human Rights Act 1998 awards of damages are discretionary; the court can find that article 2 has been violated, record the fact, but decline to award damages as a consequence. Strict time limits exist for bringing a claim under the Human Rights Act 1998 and actions must usually be brought within one year of the act which is being complained of having taken place[326].

18.3 REPORTED CASES

The majority of cases in which the ECHR finds that there has been a breach of Article 2 and awards damages for non-pecuniary loss seem to involve legal actions against the Turkish state. In the cases of *Tanrikulu v Turkey*[327], *Ogur v Turkey*[328] and *Cakici v Turkey*[329] the court found that the Turkish state had violated Article 2 and awarded varying amounts of damages to account for the relatives' non-pecuniary loss[330]. In the case of *Tanrikulu* the court explained that:

> *"...the applicant and her children have suffered non-pecuniary damage which cannot be compensated solely by the findings of*

326 See S7(5) of the Human Rights Act 1998

327 (2000) 30 E.H.R.R. 950

328 (2001) 31 E.H.R.R. 912

329 (2001) 31 E.H.R.R. 5

330 Respectively £15,000; around £10,000 and £2,500 for the applicant; and £25,000 for the deceased's heirs

violations. Making its assessment on an equitable basis, the court awards the applicant the sum of £15,000..."

Examples involving Article 2 and public authorities from the United Kingdom are more limited and proceed on a very particular set of facts. In the case of *Van Colle v Chief Constable of Hertfordshire*[331] the deceased was a witness in a trial in a relatively minor criminal matter. He was subject to a campaign of intimidation by the accused in that trial. The deceased reported this intimidation to the defendant police force who failed to act appropriately. The deceased was then murdered by the accused before the trial took place. Damages were awarded at first instance and this decision was upheld by the Court of Appeal but these decisions were reversed by the House of Lords on the basis that, according to the test set out in the case of *Osman v United Kingdom*[332] the authority could not have known (or ought not to have known) of the existence of a real and immediate threat to life.

At first instance Cox J. set out the following guidance in relation to claims relating to a breach of Article 2. These principles were approved by the Court of Appeal. They can be summarised thus:

a) Article 2 is unqualified and fundamental. Any breach requires the most anxious scrutiny by the court;

b) Nevertheless, Article 2 is not to be interpreted so as to impose an impossible or disproportionate burden on state authorities;

c) The state's positive obligation to protect life includes, in certain circumstances, a positive obligation to take preventative measures to protect an individual whose life is at risk as a result of the criminal acts of a third party;

331 [2008] UKHL 50

332 (1998) 29 E.H.R.R. 245

d) The claimant does not have to establish that the failure amounted to gross negligence or a wilful disregard of the duty to protect life. It is sufficient to show that the authorities did not do all that could reasonably be expected of them to avoid a real and immediate risk to life of which they had or ought to have had knowledge. The answer to this question will always depend on the facts of the case[333].

The case of *McCann v United Kingdom*[334] concerned the extra judicial killing of three IRA terrorists in Gibraltar by SAS soldiers. In that case the court found that there had been a breach of Article 2 but, in exercising their discretion, declined to make an award of damages on the basis that the three deceased had been intending to plant a bomb.

The case of *Keenan v United Kingdom*[335] concerned a mentally ill man who committed suicide whilst in prison. His sentence was increased whilst in prison by a further 28 days, 7 of which were served in the segregated punishment block. Although the court found that there had been a breach of Article 3[336], they did not find that Article 2 had been breached. The court did go on to award the mother of the adult child £3,000 for her non-pecuniary loss to account for the grief caused by his death.

18.4 CHALLENGES TO THE EXISTING FRAMEWORK OF LAW

As seen above there exists an extensive framework of domestic law to deal with claims for damages for fatal accidents arising out of intentional acts

333 See paragraph 56 of Van Colle v Chief Constable of Hertfordshire [2006] EWHC 360 (QB)

334 (1996) 21 E.H.R.R. 97

335 (2001) 33 E.H.R.R. 913

336 Article 3: "No one shall be subjected to torture or to inhumane or degrading treatment or punishment"

and unintentional acts (negligence). The domestic law will usually be sufficient to resolve a claim for damages following a fatal accident. The domestic legislation of the Fatal Accidents Act 1976 covers claims for pecuniary loss (claims for loss of dependency) made by dependants and also provides for non-pecuniary loss (bereavement, loss of consortium).

There remain, however, areas of the Fatal Accidents Act 1976 in relation to non-pecuniary loss (such as bereavement damages) where the strict definitions imposed by the Fatal Accidents Act 1976 exclude some claimants who seem deserving[337]. A parent whose 18 year old child dies is not entitled to a bereavement award, whereas the parent of a child who dies at 17 and 364 days is entitled. A child whose parent is killed will, almost inevitably, suffer bereavement but is not entitled to any damages for bereavement.

In these, limited, circumstances many commentators point out that a potential claim under the Human Rights Act 1998 exists where the death of the deceased has been caused by or contributed to by, a public authority. Some commentators point to the potential for further similar arguments concerning the level of funeral expenses, the level of bereavement damages; and the limited nature of the class of dependants.

A note of caution should be sounded here. In the recent cases where arguments that the existing framework of law was incompatible with the ECHR have been advanced, the arguments have been firmly rejected[338].

Overall, while the Human Rights Act 1998 remains an important consideration that cannot be ignored by the practitioner, the domestic law in this area remains by far the most likely route to a successful claim for damages.

---

337 See "Criticisms of the Current Approach" at chapter 14.5 above

338 See Thompson v Arnold op. cit. and Swift v Ministry of Justice op. cit.

18.4 SUMMARY

In summary:

a) Article 2 of the Human Rights Act 1998 sets out the "right to life";

b) Awards of damages are discretionary;

c) Strict time limits exist for bringing a claim under the Human Rights Act 1998 and actions must usually be brought within one year of the act which is being complained of having taken place;

d) Claims involving Article 2 involve a breach of duty by the state authorities which caused or contributed to the death;

e) Examples involving Article 2 and public authorities from the United Kingdom are limited and proceed on a very particular set of facts;

f) The domestic law will usually be sufficient to resolve a claim for damages following a fatal accident;

g) In the recent cases where arguments that the existing framework of law was incompatible with the ECHR have been advanced, the arguments have been firmly rejected.

CHAPTER NINETEEN

OTHER RELEVANT STATUTES

19.1 INTRODUCTION

Whilst the Fatal Accidents Act 1976 and the Law Reform (Miscellaneous) Provisions Act 1934 provide the main statutory considerations, there are other statutes which give rise to a right of action for wrongful death. In reality, the number of times that these statutes will be called into use in a practitioner's career must be vanishingly small. In this short chapter the main features of these statutes, as they relate to a claim for damages following a fatal accident, are set out.

19.2 THE COAL MINING SUBSIDENCE ACT 1991

Section 32 of the Coal Mining Subsidence Act 1991 states:

> *(1) This section applies where—*
>
> > *(a) as the result of an injury caused by the happening of subsidence damage, any person dies or is disabled (whether permanently or temporarily); and*
> >
> > *(b) apart from this section, no action to recover damages is maintainable in respect of the death or disablement.*
>
> *(2) Subject to subsection (4) below, the Corporation shall be liable, in the case of a death, to pay the like damages, recoverable in the like manner and within the like time, as would have been payable if—*

> > *(a) the death had been attributable to the negligence of the Corporation; and*
> >
> > *(b) the persons by or on behalf of whom an action could have been brought against the Corporation for damages in respect of the death if it had been so attributable included any person who at the time of the death was, or but for the injury would have been, wholly or partly maintained by the deceased; and*
> >
> > *(c) the damages were claimed under the Fatal Accidents Act 1976 where the death resulted from an injury caused in England or Wales, or the Damages (Scotland) Act 1976 Damages (Scotland) Act 2011 where the death resulted from an injury caused in Scotland.*
>
> *[...]*
>
> *(4) No liability shall attach to the Corporation under subsection (2) or (3) above in respect of the death or disablement of any person as a result of an injury if—*
>
> > *(a) at the time when that person incurred the injury he was on any land as a trespasser or, in Scotland, without lawful authority; or*
> >
> > *(b) the injury was wholly attributable to the fault of that person; and if the injury was partly attributable to the fault of that person the liability of the Corporation under that subsection shall be reduced proportionately.*

This statutory provision removes the need for the claimant dependant to prove that the deceased's death arose as a result of the wrongful act, neglect or default of the defendant where the deceased met his death as a result of subsidence damage in a coal mine in England or Wales. Section 32(2) operates so that the compensation paid across by the British Coal Corporation is assessed in line with the principles of the Fatal Accidents Act 1976. Section 32(4) removes the right of action under the Coal

Mining Subsidence Act 1991 if the deceased was a trespasser or if the injury was wholly attributable to the deceased. Section 32(4)(b) makes it clear that if there is a finding of contributory negligence on behalf of the deceased damages are reduced in the normal fashion.

19.3 RAILWAYS

The Carriage by Air Act 1961 and the Railways (Convention on International Carriage by Rail) Regulations 2005 both contain specific statutory provisions that harmonise the process of claiming damages for fatal accidents under the acts with the provisions of the Fatal Accidents Act 1976.

The Railways (Convention on International Carriage by Rail) Regulations 2005 also introduces the Uniform Rules Concerning the Contract of International Carriage of Passengers by Rail (often referred to by the shorthand "CIV"). These rules impose liability on rail carriers for loss or damage resulting in death with certain exceptions[339]. As with S32 of the Coal Mining Subsidence Act 1991 discussed above, this removes the need to prove that the death arose as a result of a wrongful act, neglect or default in the specific set of circumstances set out in that section. Any claim must be notified to the railway company within 12 months of the accident[340].

19.4 AIRCRAFT

The Carriage by Air Act 1961 brings into force the various provisions on international air travel which were initially set out in the Warsaw

339 CIV Rules Art 26

340 CIV Rules Art 60

Convention 1929 and then subsequently consolidated in the Montreal Convention 1999. Article 17 of the Montreal Convention states:

> *The carrier is liable for damage sustained in the case of death or bodily injury of a passenger upon condition only that the accident which caused the death or injury took place on board the aircraft or in the course of any of the operations of embarking or disembarking.*

As with the statutory provisions relating to coal mining and rail travel, Article 17 operates so as to remove the need to prove that the death arose as a result of a wrongful act, neglect or default in the specific circumstances described in Article 17. A full discussion of the legal definition of the terms used in Article 17 is beyond the scope of this book. Section 3 of the Carriage by Air Act 1961 states that damages are assessed in accordance with the principles of the Fatal Accidents Act 1976. Particular care must be taken in regard to limitation with accidents involving air travel. Limitation is discussed in detail in Appendix A and the principles are summarised in chapter 5.[341]

19.4 SUMMARY

In summary:

a) Section 32 of the Coal Mining Subsidence Act 1991 removes the need for the claimant dependant to prove that the deceased's death arose as a result of the wrongful act, neglect or default of the defendant where the deceased met his death as a result of subsidence damage in a coal mine in England or Wales;

b) The Railways (Convention on International Carriage by Rail) Regulations 2005 impose liability on rail carriers for loss or damage resulting in death with certain exceptions;

341 See appendix A.5 and chapter 5.6

c) The Carriage by Air Act 1961 brings into force article 17 of the Montreal Convention which remove the need to prove that the death arose as a result of a wrongful act, neglect or default in the specific circumstances described therein.

APPENDIX A

LIMITATION

A.1 INTRODUCTION

As with all litigation, limitation is an important consideration. A full discussion of the area of limitation is beyond the scope of this book and other excellent specialist textbooks exist. What follows below is a discussion of the key principles of limitation as they pertain to claims arising out of fatal accidents.

A.2. SECTION 11 OF THE LIMITATION ACT 1980

Section 11 of the Limitation Act 1980 sets out a primary limitation period of three years for actions under the Fatal Accidents Act 1976 and the Law Reform (Miscellaneous Provisions) Act 1934. It states:

> *11 Special time limit for actions in respect of personal injuries.*
>
> *(1) This section applies to any action for damages for negligence, nuisance or breach of duty (whether the duty exists by virtue of a contract or of provision made by or under a statute or independently of any contract or any such provision) where the damages claimed by the plaintiff for the negligence, nuisance or breach of duty consist of or include damages in respect of personal injuries to the plaintiff or any other person.*
>
> *(1A) This section does not apply to any action brought for damages under section 3 of the Protection from Harassment Act 1997.*
>
> *(2) None of the time limits given in the preceding provisions of this Act shall apply to an action to which this section applies.*

(3) An action to which this section applies shall not be brought after the expiration of the period applicable in accordance with subsection (4) or (5) below.

(4) Except where subsection (5) below applies, the period applicable is three years from—

(a) the date on which the cause of action accrued; or

(b) the date of knowledge (if later) of the person injured.

(5) If the person injured dies before the expiration of the period mentioned in subsection (4) above, the period applicable as respects the cause of action surviving for the benefit of his estate by virtue of section 1 of the Law Reform (Miscellaneous Provisions) Act 1934 shall be three years from—

(a) the date of death; or

(b) the date of the personal representative's knowledge; whichever is the later.

(6) For the purposes of this section "personal representative" includes any person who is or has been a personal representative of the deceased, including an executor who has not proved the will (whether or not he has renounced probate) but not anyone appointed only as a special personal representative in relation to settled land; and regard shall be had to any knowledge acquired by any such person while a personal representative or previously.

(7) If there is more than one personal representative, and their dates of knowledge are different, subsection (5)(b) above shall be read as referring to the earliest of those dates.

A.3 SECTION 12 OF THE LIMITATION ACT 1980

Section 12 of the Limitation Act sets out how limitation operates in the context of claims under the Fatal Accidents Act legislation. It states:

> *12 Special time limit for actions under Fatal Accidents legislation.*
>
> *(1) An action under the Fatal Accidents Act 1976 shall not be brought if the death occurred when the person injured could no longer maintain an action and recover damages in respect of the injury (whether because of a time limit in this Act or in any other Act, or for any other reason).*
>
> *Where any such action by the injured person would have been barred by the time limit in section 11 or 11A of this Act, no account shall be taken of the possibility of that time limit being overridden under section 33 of this Act.*
>
> *(2) None of the time limits given in the preceding provisions of this Act shall apply to an action under the Fatal Accidents Act 1976, but no such action shall be brought after the expiration of three years from—*
>
> > *(a) the date of death; or*
> >
> > *(b) the date of knowledge of the person for whose benefit the action is brought; whichever is the later.*
>
> *(3) An action under the Fatal Accidents Act 1976 shall be one to which sections 28, 33 and 35 of this Act apply, and the application to any such action of the time limit under subsection (2) above shall be subject to section 39; but otherwise Parts II and III of this Act shall not apply to any such action.*

Particular care should be exercised where the deceased has suffered an injury and then died some time afterwards. Any claim needs to be advanced within three years of the deceased's date of knowledge.

A.4 ACCIDENTS AT SEA

In relation to passengers at sea S183 of the Merchant Shipping Act 1995 incorporates the Athens Convention 1974 into UK law. The Athens Convention prescribes a strict two year time limit for bringing claims for personal injury and death that occur at sea. There is no possibility of extending this limitation period. The period of time is calculated from disembarkation. If the death occurs after disembarkation the two year period runs from the time of death but any claim must be brought within three years of disembarkation.

In relation to actions arising out of the collision of vessels the Maritime Conventions Act 1911 applies. This also applies a two year limitation period. This period does not apply if:

a) The vessel was not "in the course of navigation" when the collision occurred[342];

b) The accident was caused by the negligence of an individual on the vessel on which the deceased was sailing[343].

A.5 ACCIDENTS IN THE AIR

In relation to accidents on air travel particular care should be exercised. The provisions of the Montreal Convention are incorporated into English law by the Carriage by Air Act 1961[344]. Article 35 of the Montreal Convention prescribes a strict two year limitation period. This period is absolute and cannot be extended by operation of S33 of the Limitation Act. The scope of the Convention is a broad one and applies

342 Curtis v Wild [1991] 4 All ER 172

343 Navarro v Larrinaga Steamship Co Ltd [1966] P 80

344 As amended by the Carriage by Air Acts (Implementation of the Montreal Convention 1999) Order 2002

to a wide variety of aircraft[345] and can be extended to encompass accidents that occur while embarking and disembarking the aircraft and accidents that occur in the airport itself.[346]

A.6 ACCIDENTS ABROAD

Care should also be exercised in relation to accidents that occurred abroad. The Foreign Limitation Periods Act 1984 states:

> *(1) Subject to the following provisions of this Act, where in any action or proceedings in a court in England and Wales the law of any other country falls (in accordance with rules of private international law applicable by any such court) to be taken into account in the determination of any matter—*
>
> *(a) the law of that other country relating to limitation shall apply in respect of that matter for the purposes of the action or proceedings; and*
>
> *(b) except where that matter falls within subsection (2) below, the law of England and Wales relating to limitation shall not so apply.*

Section 2 of the Act allows an exception to this rule if applying the foreign limitation period conflict with public policy or creates undue hardship. However, these exceptions are interpreted strictly by the courts.

A.7 THE OPERATION OF SECTION 33 OF THE LIMITATION ACT 1980

As we have seen above S12 of the Limitation Act 1980 states that S33 of the Limitation Act applies to claims for fatal accidents. Section 33 of the

345 Michael Laroche v Spirit of Adventure (UK) Ltd [2008] EWHC 788 (QB)

346 Adatia v Air Canada [1992] PIQR P238

Limitation Act allows the court to dis-apply the primary limitation period if the court views it as equitable to do so. As discussed above the court has no power to dis-apply the primary limitation period imposed by Montreal Convention or the Athens Convention. A full discussion of the operation of S33 is beyond the scope of this book.

A.8 SUMMARY

In summary:

a) Where death is immediate the limitation period is usually 3 years;

b) Where the deceased was a minor the limitation period runs from their 18th birthday or from the date of death (whichever is sooner);

c) Where a dependant is a child their limitation period does not start to run until they are 18;

d) If the deceased was mentally incapable of bringing an action between the accident and the date of the death then the limitation period did not start to run in the deceased's lifetime;

e) Where the deceased has survived for a period of time after the accident and then died a new three year limitation period commences on the day of death;

f) If the deceased survived for a period of longer than 3 years and no action was commenced then any action by his dependants after his death is time barred;

g) Particular care must be taken in regard to accidents at sea and accidents involving aircraft where, in certain circumstances, the limitation period is a strict 2 years;

h) Particular care must be taken if the accident has occurred abroad as the limitation period which prevails is the period of limitation in the accident where the accident occurs.

i) An application can be made under S33 of the Limitation Act 1980 to extend the limitation period. This application cannot be made in cases where the cause of action is under the Montreal Convention (accidents involving air travel) or the Athens Convention (accidents at sea).

APPENDIX B

FATAL ACCIDENTS ACT 1976

[F1 1 Right of action for wrongful act causing death.

(1) If death is caused by any wrongful act, neglect or default which is such as would (if death had not ensued) have entitled the person injured to maintain an action and recover damages in respect thereof, the person who would have been liable if death had not ensued shall be liable to an action for damages, notwithstanding the death of the person injured.

(2) Subject to section 1A(2) below, every such action shall be for the benefit of the dependants of the person ("the deceased") whose death has been so caused.

(3) In this Act "dependant" means—

(a) the wife or husband or former wife or husband of the deceased;

[F2(aa) the civil partner or former civil partner of the deceased;]

(b) any person who—

(i) was living with the deceased in the same household immediately before the date of the death; and

(ii) had been living with the deceased in the same household for at least two years before that date; and

(iii) was living during the whole of that period as the husband or wife[F3or civil partner] of the deceased;

(c) any parent or other ascendant of the deceased;

(d) any person who was treated by the deceased as his parent;

(e) any child or other descendant of the deceased;

(f) any person (not being a child of the deceased) who, in the case of any marriage to which the deceased was at any time a party, was treated by the deceased as a child of the family in relation to that marriage;

[F4(fa) any person (not being a child of the deceased) who, in the case of any civil partnership in which the deceased was at any time a civil partner, was treated by the deceased as a child of the family in relation to that civil partnership;]

(g) any person who is, or is the issue of, a brother, sister, uncle or aunt of the deceased.

(4) The reference to the former wife or husband of the deceased in subsection (3)(a) above includes a reference to a person whose marriage to the deceased has been annulled or declared void as well as a person whose marriage to the deceased has been dissolved.

[F5(4A) The reference to the former civil partner of the deceased in subsection (3)(aa) above includes a reference to a person whose civil partnership with the deceased has been annulled as well as a person whose civil partnership with the deceased has been dissolved.]

(5) In deducing any relationship for the purposes of subsection (3) above—

(a) any relationship [F6by marriage or civil partnership] shall be treated as a relationship by consanguinity, any relationship of the half blood as a relationship of the whole blood, and the stepchild of any person as his child, and

[F7(b) an illegitimate person shall be treated as—

(i) the legitimate child of his mother and reputed father, or

(ii) in the case of a person who has a female parent by virtue of section 43 of the Human Fertilisation and Embryology Act 2008, the legitimate child of his mother and that female parent.]

(6) Any reference in this Act to injury includes any disease and any impairment of a person's physical or mental condition.]

1A Bereavement.

(1) An action under this Act may consist of or include a claim for damages for bereavement.

(2) A claim for damages for bereavement shall only be for the benefit—

(a) of the wife or husband[F1or civil partner] of the deceased; and

(b) where the deceased was a minor who was never married[F2or a civil partner]—

(i) of his parents, if he was legitimate; and

(ii) of his mother, if he was illegitimate.

(3) Subject to subsection (5) below, the sum to be awarded as damages under this section shall be [F3 £12,980].

(4) Where there is a claim for damages under this section for the benefit of both the parents of the deceased, the sum awarded shall be divided equally between them (subject to any deduction falling to be made in respect of costs not recovered from the defendant).

(5) The Lord Chancellor may by order made by statutory instrument, subject to annulment in pursuance of a resolution of either House of Parliament, amend this section by varying the sum for the time being specified in subsection (3) above.

2 Persons entitled to bring the action.

(1) The action shall be brought by and in the name of the executor or administrator of the deceased.

(2) If—

(a) there is no executor or administrator of the deceased, or

(b) no action is brought within six months after the death by and in the name of an executor or administrator of the deceased,

the action may be brought by and in the name of all or any of the persons for whose benefit an executor or administrator could have brought it.

(3) Not more than one action shall lie for and in respect of the same subject matter of complaint.

(4) The plaintiff in the action shall be required to deliver to the defendant or his solicitor full particulars of the persons for whom and on whose behalf the action is brought and of the nature of the claim in respect of which damages are sought to be recovered.

3 Assessment of damages.

(1) In the action such damages, other than damages for bereavement, may be awarded as are proportioned to the injury resulting from the death to the dependants respectively.

(2) After deducting the costs not recovered from the defendant any amount recovered otherwise than as damages for bereavement shall be divided among the dependants in such shares as may be directed.

(3) In an action under this Act where there fall to be assessed damages payable to a widow in respect of the death of her husband there shall not be taken account the re-marriage of the widow or her prospects of re-marriage.

(4) In an action under this Act where there fall to be assessed damages payable to a person who is a dependant by virtue of section 1(3)(b) above in respect of the death of the person with whom the dependant was living as husband or wife[F1or civil partner] there shall be taken into account (together with any other matter that appears to the court to be relevant to the action) the fact that the dependant had no enforceable right to financial support by the deceased as a result of their living together.

(5) If the dependants have incurred funeral expenses in respect of the deceased, damages may be awarded in respect of those expenses.

(6) Money paid into court in satisfaction of a cause of action under this Act may be in one sum without specifying any person's share.

4 Assessment of damages: disregard of benefits.

In assessing damages in respect of a person's death in an action under this Act, benefits which have accrued or may accrue to any person from his estate or otherwise as a result of his death shall be disregarded.

5 Contributory negligence.

Where any person dies as the result partly of his own fault and partly of the fault of any other person or persons, and accordingly if an action were brought for the benefit of the estate under the M1Law Reform (Miscellaneous Provisions) Act 1934 the damages recoverable would be reduced under section 1(1) of the M2Law Reform (Contributory Negligence) Act 1945, any damages recoverable in an action . . . F1 under this Act shall be reduced to a proportionate extent.

6 Consequential amendments and repeals.

(1) Schedule 1 to this Act contains consequential amendments.

(2) The enactments specified in Schedule 2 to this Act are repealed to the extent specified in the third column of that Schedule.

7 Short title, etc.

(1) This Act may be cited as the Fatal Accidents Act 1976.

(2) This Act shall come into force on 1st September 1976, but shall not apply to any cause of action arising on a death before it comes into force.

(3) This Act shall not extend to Scotland or Northern Ireland.

Source: http://www.legislation.gov.uk/ukpga/1976/30/contents

APPENDIX C

LAW REFORM (MISCELLANEOUS PROVISIONS) ACT 1934

1 Effect of death on certain causes of action.

(1) Subject to the provisions of this section, on the death of any person after the commencement of this Act all causes of action subsisting against or vested in him shall survive against, or, as the case may be, for the benefit of, his estate. Provided that this subsection shall not apply to causes of action for defamation.

(1A) The right of a person to claim under section 1A of the Fatal Accidents Act 1976 (bereavement) shall not survive for the benefit of his estate on his death.

(2) Where a cause of action survives as aforesaid for the benefit of the estate of a deceased person, the damages recoverable for the benefit of the estate of that person—

(a) shall not include—

(i) any exemplary damages;

(ii) any damages for loss of income in respect of any period after that person's death;]

(b) . . . . . .

(c) Where the death of that person has been caused by the act or omission which gives rise to the cause of action, shall be calculated without

reference to any loss or gain to his estate consequent on his death, exept that a sum in respect of funeral expenses may be included.

(3) . . .

(4) Where damage has been suffered by reason of any act or omission in respect of which a cause of action would have subsisted against any person if that person had not died before or at the same time as the damage was suffered, there shall be deemed, for the purposes of this Act, to have been subsisting against him before his death such cause of action in respect of that act or omission as would have subsisted if he had died after the damage was suffered.

(5) The rights conferred by this Act for the benefit of the estates of deceased persons shall be in addition to and not in derogation of any rights conferred on the dependants of deceased persons by the Fatal Accidents Acts 1846 to 1908, . . . and so much of this Act as relates to causes of action against the estates of deceased persons shall apply in relation to causes of action under the said Acts as it applies in relation to other causes of action not expressly excepted from the operation of subsection (1) of this section.

(6) In the event of the insolvency of an estate against which proceedings are maintainable by virtue of this section, any liability in respect of the cause of action in respect of which the proceedings are maintainable shall be deemed to be a debt provable in the administration of the estate, notwithstanding that it is a demand in the nature of unliquidated damages arising otherwise than by a contract, promise or breach of trust.

(7) . . .

2. . . . .

3 Power of courts of record to award interest on debts and damages.

(1) In any proceedings tried in any court of record for the recovery of any debt or damages, the court may, if it thinks fit, order that there shall be included in the sum for which judgment is given interest at such rate as it thinks fit on the whole or any part of the debt or damages for the whole or any part of the period between the date when the cause of action arose and the date of the judgment:

Provided that nothing in this section—

> *(a) shall authorise the giving of interest upon interest; or*
>
> *(b) shall apply in relation to any debt upon which interest is payable as of right whether by virtue of any agreement or otherwise; or*
>
> *(c) shall affect the damages recoverable for the dishonour of a bill of exchange.*

(1A) Where in any such proceedings as are mentioned in subsection (1) of this section judgment is given for a sum which (apart from interest on damages) exceeds £200 and represents or includes damages in respect of personal injuries to the plaintiff or any other person, or in respect of a person's death, then (without prejudice to the exercise of the power conferred by that subsection in relation to any part of that sum which does not represent such damages) the court shall exercise that power so as to include in that sum interest on those damages or on such part of them as the court considers appropriate, unless the court is satisfied that there are special reasons why no interest should be given in respect of those damages.

(1B) Any order under this section may provide for interest to be calculated at different rates in respect of different parts of the period for which interest is given, whether that period is the whole or part of the period mentioned in subsection (1) of this section.

(1C) . . . .

(1D) In this section "personal injuries' includes any disease and any impairment of a person's physical or mental condition, ...

(2) . . .

4 Short title and extent.

(1) —This Act may be cited as the Law Reform (Miscellaneous Provisions) Act 1934.

(2) This Act shall not extend to Scotland or Northern Ireland.

Source: http://www.legislation.gov.uk/ukpga/Geo5/24-25/41/contents

MORE BOOKS BY LAW BRIEF PUBLISHING

A selection of our other titles available now:-

'A Practical Guide to Probation Breaches and Other Applications' by Mark Thomas
'A Practical Guide to Remarriage and Divorce' by Cordelia Williams & Claire Howard
'A Practical Guide to Privacy, Transparency, Reporting Restrictions and Closed Proceedings in the Court of Protection' by Laura Mannering
'Beaumont on Barristers – A Guide to Defending Disciplinary Proceedings (Second Edition)' by Marc Beaumont
'A Practical Guide to Payments for Environmental Services' by Ben Sharples
'A Practical Guide to the Law of Pregnancy and Maternity at Work' by Rebecca Thomas
'A Practical Guide to Redundancy – Second Edition' by Philip Hyland & Collette Moore
'A Practical Guide to International Issues for Scottish Family Lawyers' by Susie Mountain, Donna McKay, Ken MacDonald
'A Practical Guide to the Law on Deprivation of Liberty' by Ben Troke
'A Practical Guide to Rights over Airspace and Subsoil – Second Edition' by Daniel Gatty
'A Practical Guide to the Law in Relation to Inquests' by Ramya Nagesh
'A Practical Guide to the Construction and Rectification of Wills and Trust Instruments (Second Edition)' by Edward Hewitt
'A Practical Guide to Data Protection in Social Housing' by Clare Paterson
'A Practical Guide to Spousal Maintenance – Second Edition' by Liz Cowell
'A Practical Guide to International Parental Child Abduction Law (England and Wales)' by Dr Onyója Momoh
'A Practical Guide to Deprivation of British Citizenship' by Sean Ell
'A Practical Guide to Commercial Property Service Charges' by Rachel Garton
'A Practical Guide to Clinical Negligence – Third Edition' by Geoffrey Simpson-Scott (Geoff)
'A Practical Guide to the Rights of Grandparents in Children Proceedings – Second Edition' by Stuart Barlow

'The Electronic Communications Code: A Practical Guide – Second Edition' by Kerry Bretherton KC, James Castle, Mark Loveday
'A Practical Guide to the Independent School Standards – September 2023 Edition' by Sarah McKimm
'A Practical Guide to Estate Administration and Crypto Assets' by Richard Marshall
'A Practical Guide to Parental Alienation in Private and Public Law Children Cases' by Sam King QC & Frankie Shama
'Contested Heritage – Removing Art from Land and Historic Buildings' by Richard Harwood QC, Catherine Dobson, David Sawtell
'The Limits of Separate Legal Personality: When Those Running a Company Can Be Held Personally Liable for Losses Caused to Third Parties Outside of the Company' by Dr Mike Wilkinson
'A Practical Guide to Transgender Law' by Robin Moira White & Nicola Newbegin
'A Practical Guide to 'Stranded Spouses' in Family Law' by Mani Singh Basi
'A Practical Guide to Residential Freehold Conveyancing' by Lorraine Richardson
'A Practical Guide to Pensions on Divorce for Lawyers' by Bryan Scant
'A Practical Guide to Challenging Sham Marriage Allegations in Immigration Law' by Priya Solanki
'A Practical Guide to Digital Communications Evidence in Criminal Law' by Sam Willis
'A Practical Guide to Legal Rights in Scotland' by Sarah-Jane Macdonald
'A Practical Guide to New Build Conveyancing' by Paul Sams & Rebecca East
'A Practical Guide to Inherited Wealth on Divorce' by Hayley Trim
'A Practical Guide to Practice Direction 12J and Domestic Abuse in Private Law Children Proceedings' by Rebecca Cross & Malvika Jaganmohan
'A Practical Guide to Confiscation and Restraint' by Narita Bahra QC, John Carl Townsend, David Winch
'A Practical Guide to the Law of Forests in Scotland' by Philip Buchan
'A Practical Guide to Health and Medical Cases in Immigration Law' by Rebecca Chapman & Miranda Butler
'A Practical Guide to Bad Character Evidence for Criminal Practitioners by Aparna Rao
'A Practical Guide to Extradition Law post-Brexit' by Myles Grandison et al
'A Practical Guide to Hoarding and Mental Health for Housing Lawyers' by Rachel Coyle

'Stephens on Contractual Indemnities' by Richard Stephens
'A Practical Guide to the EU Succession Regulation' by Richard Frimston
'A Practical Guide to Solicitor and Client Costs – Second Edition' by Robin Dunne
'Constructive Dismissal – Practice Pointers and Principles' by Benjimin Burgher
'A Practical Guide to Religion and Belief Discrimination Claims in the Workplace' by Kashif Ali
'A Practical Guide to the Law of Medical Treatment Decisions' by Ben Troke
'Fundamental Dishonesty and QOCS in Personal Injury Proceedings: Law and Practice' by Jake Rowley
'A Practical Guide to the Law in Relation to School Exclusions' by Charlotte Hadfield & Alice de Coverley
'A Practical Guide to Divorce for the Silver Separators' by Karin Walker
'The Right to be Forgotten – The Law and Practical Issues' by Melissa Stock
'A Practical Guide to Planning Law and Rights of Way in National Parks, the Broads and AONBs' by James Maurici QC, James Neill et al
'A Practical Guide to Election Law' by Tom Tabori
'A Practical Guide to the Law in Relation to Surrogacy' by Andrew Powell
'A Practical Guide to Claims Arising from Fatal Accidents – Second Edition' by James Patience
'A Practical Guide to Asbestos Claims' by Jonathan Owen & Gareth McAloon
'A Practical Guide to Stamp Duty Land Tax in England and Northern Ireland' by Suzanne O'Hara
'A Practical Guide to the Law of Farming Partnerships' by Philip Whitcomb
'A Practical Guide to the Law of Unlawful Eviction and Harassment – Second Edition' by Stephanie Lovegrove
'A Practical Guide to Costs in Personal Injury Claims – Second Edition' by Matthew Hoe
'A Practical Guide to the General Data Protection Regulation (GDPR) – Second Edition' by Keith Markham
'A Practical Guide to Working with Litigants in Person and McKenzie Friends in Family Cases' by Stuart Barlow
'Protecting Unregistered Brands: A Practical Guide to the Law of Passing Off' by Lorna Brazell
'A Practical Guide to Secondary Liability and Joint Enterprise Post-Jogee' by Joanne Cecil & James Mehigan

'A Practical Guide to the Pre-Action RTA Claims Protocol for Personal Injury Lawyers' by Antonia Ford
'A Practical Guide to Neighbour Disputes and the Law' by Alexander Walsh
'A Practical Guide to Coercive Control for Legal Practitioners and Victims' by Rachel Horman
'A Practical Guide to the Law of Driverless Cars – Second Edition'
by Alex Glassbrook, Emma Northey & Scarlett Milligan
'A Practical Guide to TOLATA Claims' by Greg Williams
'A Practical Guide to Elderly Law – Second Edition' by Justin Patten
'A Practical Guide to Responding to Housing Disrepair and Unfitness Claims' by Iain Wightwick
'A Practical Guide to the Law of Bullying and Harassment in the Workplace' by Philip Hyland
'How to Be a Freelance Solicitor: A Practical Guide to the SRA-Regulated Freelance Solicitor Model' by Paul Bennett
'A Practical Guide to Prison Injury Claims' by Malcolm Johnson
'A Practical Guide to Advising Clients at the Police Station' by Colin Stephen McKeown-Beaumont
'A Practical Guide to Antisocial Behaviour Injunctions – Second Edition' by Iain Wightwick
'Practical Mediation: A Guide for Mediators, Advocates, Advisers, Lawyers, and Students in Civil, Commercial, Business, Property, Workplace, and Employment Cases' by Jonathan Dingle with John Sephton
'The Mini-Pupillage Workbook' by David Boyle
'A Practical Guide to Crofting Law' by Brian Inkster
'A Practical Guide to the Law of Domain Names and Cybersquatting' by Andrew Clemson
'A Practical Guide to the Law of Gender Pay Gap Reporting' by Harini Iyengar
'NHS Whistleblowing and the Law' by Joseph England
'Employment Law and the Gig Economy' by Nigel Mackay & Annie Powell
'A Practical Guide to Noise Induced Hearing Loss (NIHL) Claims' by Andrew Mckie, Ian Skeate, Gareth McAloon
'An Introduction to Beauty Negligence Claims – A Practical Guide for the Personal Injury Practitioner' by Greg Almond
'Intercompany Agreements for Transfer Pricing Compliance' by Paul Sutton
'Zen and the Art of Mediation' by Martin Plowman
'A Practical Guide to Adoption for Family Lawyers' by Graham Pegg

‘A Practical Guide to Industrial Disease Claims’ by Andrew Mckie & Ian Skeate
‘A Practical Guide to Conducting a Sheriff Court Proof’ by Andrew Stevenson
‘A Practical Guide to Vicarious Liability’ by Mariel Irvine
‘A Practical Guide to Applications for Landlord’s Consent and Variation of Leases’ by Mark Shelton
‘A Practical Guide to Relief from Sanctions Post-Mitchell and Denton’ by Peter Causton
‘A Practical Guide to Equity Release for Advisors’ by Paul Sams
‘A Practical Guide to Financial Services Claims’ by Chris Hegarty
‘A Practical Guide to Financial Ombudsman Service Claims’ by Adam Temple & Robert Scrivenor
‘A Practical Guide to Running Housing Disrepair and Cavity Wall Claims – Second Edition’ by Andrew Mckie & Ian Skeate
‘A Practical Guide to Holiday Sickness Claims – Second Edition’ by Andrew Mckie & Ian Skeate
‘Arguments and Tactics for Personal Injury and Clinical Negligence Claims’ by Dorian Williams
‘A Practical Guide to Drone Law’ by Rufus Ballaster, Andrew Firman, Eleanor Clot
‘On Experts: CPR35 for Lawyers and Experts’ by David Boyle
‘An Introduction to Personal Injury Law’ by David Boyle

These books and more are available to order online direct from the publisher at www.lawbriefpublishing.com, where you can also read free sample chapters. For any queries, call us on 0844 587 2383 or email us at mail@lawbriefpublishing.com.

Our books are all generally in stock at www.amazon.co.uk with free next day delivery for Prime members, and at good legal bookshops such as Wildy & Sons.

We are regularly launching new books in our series of practical day-to-day practitioners' guides. Visit our website and join our free newsletter to be kept informed and to receive special offers, free chapters, etc.

You can also follow us on Twitter at www.twitter.com/lawbriefpub.

www.ingramcontent.com/pod-product-compliance
Lightning Source LLC
LaVergne TN
LVHW052322200926
848481LV00002B/636
9781918241266